8 KEYS TO
BRAIN–BODY BALANCE

8 Keys to Mental Health Series

Babette Rothschild, Series Editor

The 8 Keys series of books provides consumers with brief, inexpensive, and high-quality self-help books on a variety of topics in mental health. Each volume is written by an expert in the field, someone who is capable of presenting evidence-based information in a concise and clear way. These books stand out by offering consumers cutting-edge, relevant theory in easily digestible portions, written in an accessible style. The tone is respectful of the reader and the messages are immediately applicable. Filled with exercises and practical strategies, these books empower readers to help themselves.

8 KEYS TO BRAIN–BODY BALANCE

ROBERT SCAER, MD

Foreword by Babette Rothschild

W. W. Norton & Company

New York · London

For information about permission to reproduce selections from this book,
write to Permissions, W. W. Norton & Company, Inc.,
500 Fifth Avenue, New York, NY 10110

For information about special discounts for bulk purchases,
please contact W. W. Norton Special Sales at
specialsales@wwnorton.com or 800-233-4830

Manufacturing by R.R. Donnelley-Harrisonburg
Production manager: Leeann Graham

Library of Congress Cataloging-in-Publication Data

Scaer, Robert C.
   8 keys to brain-body balance / Robert Scaer ; foreword
by Babette Rothschild. — 1st ed.
      p. cm.
   Includes bibliographical references and index.
   ISBN 978-0-393-70747-2 (pbk.)
1. Mind and body.   2. Mind and body
therapies.   3. Stress (Psychology)   4. Psychic
trauma.   5. Mental healing.   I. Title.   II. Title: Eight
keys to brain-body balance.
   BF161.S25 2012
   158.1—dc23   2012014863

ISBN: 978-0-393-70747-2 (pbk.)

W. W. Norton & Company, Inc., 500 Fifth Avenue, New York, N.Y. 10110
www.wwnorton.com
W. W. Norton & Company Ltd., Castle House, 75/76 Wells Street,
London W1T 3QT

1 2 3 4 5 6 7 8 9 0

Contents

Foreword

Traditionally, science and psychology have considered the brain and body to be separate, in the same vein as Descartes' proposal of "I think therefore I am." However, increasingly, many involved in neuroscience and psychology have come to recognize that the body and brain, including the mind, are inseparably linked, that they interact constantly and on all levels including emotions, decision making, and all sorts of psychological and physical processes.

Basically, the brain is at the center of the universe that is the body; the brain is, indeed, part of the body. It is physically and functionally placed at the center of the central nervous system, the center of the entire nervous system of the body. All of our body processes as well as our awareness of those processes—senses, movement, appetites, instincts, skills, thoughts, feelings, and so on—would not exist in the absence of a brain. It is truly an amazing and somewhat mysterious organ and its relationship with the body is awe-inspiring. How it directs and interacts with the body has been a focus of study and speculation for thousands of years. In recent times, brain science and knowledge has accelerated at a rapid pace. What we have learned about the brain to date has more than doubled in just the last few decades.

Unfortunately for the majority of us, most of the scientific writing about the brain and body is in terms that few but the most scientifically oriented can understand. I have been looking for a long time for a book on brain and body that my clients could understand and my students make use of. Enter author Robert C. Scaer. One of his many talents is transforming complicated science into accessible science. I think of him as "The Science Guy" of neuroscience. His two previous books, *The Body Bears the Burden* and *The Trauma Spectrum*, have been widely appreciated for their accessibility and insights. Early in his medical career, Scaer specialized in neurology both as a practitioner and as a clinical professor and he holds a certificate as a Diplomat of the American Board of Psychiatry and Neurology. His theoretical background as well as hands-on experience as a specialist in brain injury, chronic pain, and traumatic stress make for a particularly authoritative blend.

The reader interested in gaining a greater understanding of the brain and body, their relationship and inter-workings, is in for a treat. Scaer's book, 8 Keys to Brain–Body Balance, is full of enlightening and easy-to-digest information. As well, there are plenty of insights and exercises that make the theory come alive while enhancing the reader's own brain and body balance. Scaer makes particular use of his experience in working with patients whose brains and bodies are severely out of balance, including those suffering from stress, traumatic stress, and chronic pain. He emphasizes the hopeful fact that brain wiring can be changed and offers useful tools for improving function.

8 Keys to Brain–Body Balance, though full of cutting-edge theory, is not a heady scientific text or treatise. This is a book from one human with a brain and body written purposefully to other humans with brains and bodies. The alienation many of us feel from the one or the other can be healed by learning to listen to both. That said, Scaer in no way loses sight of the complexities he is dealing with, stirring our curiosity while gently challenging us to take concrete steps. This book will be a useful reference for readers whose main interest is in increasing their knowledge about the brain. Its even greater value will be for those who are suffering from the effects of disharmony in the brain/body relationship. With this book, there is help, relief, and healing to be had. I am so enthusiastic about this addition to the 8 Keys Series that I will be adding it to the required reading lists of my own courses and trainings in Somatic Trauma Therapy. It will provide my students with clarification and understanding of concepts and processes that have, until now, long eluded them.

The 8 Keys Self-Help Series aims, among other things, to empower readers to be in charge of their well-being and (where necessary) their healing, whether or not they are utilizing self-help or engaging the services of a helping professional. One of the tools that facilitates confidence in taking those reins is knowledge. Gathering information relevant to whatever issues you are dealing with will enhance your understanding and put you in a better position to evaluate advice you are being given and make your own decisions. Theory—and in the case of psychotherapy, neuroscientific theory—is a particularly powerful resource in this regard. The more you understand about your brain and your body, how they function together and how you can improve their interaction, the better you will be able to help and advocate for yourself.

That is why 8 *Keys to Brain–Body Balance*, as well as all of the other books in the 8 Keys Series, highlights the latest available theory and research. The result is a series of intelligent self-help books that not only instruct but also inform.

Babette Rothschild
8 Keys Series Editor
Author of *The Body Remembers*

Preface

When I was asked to write a short, user-friendly book as part of W. W. Norton's "8 Key" series, edited by Babette Rothschild and Deborah Malmud, I responded that, although I'm a clinical neurologist, I'm not a psychotherapist trained in the treatment skills required to provide therapy for trauma patients. My late-life career path into the field of traumatic stress and its consequences was triggered by my long career as a rehabilitation neurologist, treating patients with a wide variety of physical and neurological disabilities. As such, I observed the predictable emotional distress associated with physical and cognitive impairments, especially chronic pain. My personal contact with my Colorado neighbor, Peter Levine, a prominent psychologist in the field of life trauma, opened up for me a whole new concept of the way the brain works in trauma, as well as how it may lead to a host of medical syndromes that otherwise seem inexplicable or even counterintuitive. Applying to my own patients the principles of the neurophysiology of trauma developed by many pioneers in the field of posttraumatic stress disorder (PTSD), I first presented several new concepts about how the brain works in trauma in my 2001 book *The Body Bears the Burden*. I've subsequently seen hundreds of patients with PTSD and other manifestations of trauma, not as a therapist, but as an interpreter of their symptoms, an educator, and a source of referral to therapists skilled in the treatment of trauma.

Because my formal training has been in the workings of the brain in health, illness, and injury, I was convinced by my Norton colleagues to write about the brain from my point of view as a neurologist clinician and neurophysiologist, providing a clear, easy-to-understand discussion of its inner workings in health and disease. Widespread interest in the brain has emerged in popular literature, primarily due to an explosion of knowledge in the field—knowledge that has overturned decades of previous assumptions. This enlightenment has led to the vast growth of psychopharmacology, the use of drugs for the treatment of mental disorders. It has also led to the recognition that the physical symptoms of emotional disorders are not "imaginary" but rather are actual physical disorders of the body that reflect the brain's physiology in trauma.

This new understanding of the body's role in creating and perpetuating the symptoms of trauma has led to the incorporation of body processes into trauma therapy, a field that I have chosen to call somatic psychotherapy. Many of these therapies have developed from the observations of therapists, who noticed correlations between specific physical actions of the therapist and sudden improvements in their patients' symptoms. Others have evolved from a logical extension of the protocol for a specific therapy, or from discovering increased effectiveness with a minor manipulation of the technique.

Somatic psychotherapy involves sometimes-ritualistic behaviors such as moving the eyes back and forth, experiencing alternating left-right sounds or vibratory sensations, tapping on acupuncture meridian points on the head and body while verbalizing affirmative statements, or following the slow movement of a wand around one's peripheral vision. These body-based trauma therapies are a dramatic departure from traditional cognitive psychotherapy, and they have been met with skepticism by traditional psychotherapists, who criticize them for not being "evidence-based." But their popularity has grown exponentially due to the enthusiastic claims of their effectiveness by a large portion of the trauma-therapy community, and they have become part of the therapeutic repertoire of many thousands of therapists. I will make an effort to explore the basic elements of these therapies, and try to provide a physiological rationale for how they indeed may work.

Book Structure

This book, organized into four parts, contains a total of eight chapters, or "Keys."

Part I addresses the brain mechanisms for sensing the internal and external worlds and responding to them.

Key 1 introduces the basic mechanisms of the brain that access sensations of the environment through the sensory receptors of the head and body. It also explains sensory messages that arise from our body, primarily from the *viscera*, or organs of the chest and abdomen, commonly referred to as the "gut." Finally, it looks into the functions of our "thinking, verbal, deductive" left brain and our "intuitive, feeling, spatial" right brain.

Key 2 analyzes how responses to external and internal sensory systems are organized through motor memory. It also discusses the acquisition of skills for both motor performance and survival.

Part II explores the functions of the unconscious brain.

Key 3 details the functions of the autonomic nervous system, the master regulator of the endocrine and gut functions that sustain stability and homeostasis. It specifically analyzes the fight/flight sympathetic nervous system, and the vegetative, rest/restore parasympathetic nervous system.

Key 4 reviews the functions of our limbic system, also known as the "mammalian" or "emotional" brain. This complex structure governs the critical functions of arousal, memory, affiliation and bonding, and systems of reward and pleasure.

Part III addresses abnormal responses of all of these systems to negative life events and experiences.

Key 5 details the latest evidence for the plasticity and malleability of the brain, a topic of increasing interest and discovery. We'll learn that plasticity may have both positive and negative consequences.

Key 6 analyzes the effects of life stress and trauma on the brain and the autonomic nervous system, and it provides a rationale for many of the symptoms of trauma, PTSD, and dissociation.

Key 7 looks at the same issues of stress and trauma as they affect the body. We'll see not only how stress and trauma may be quite different in the physical diseases and syndromes they cause, but also how they share a significant interface and blending of the physical ailments they cause.

Part IV addresses how we can heal the brain and body in stress and trauma.

Key 8 looks at a theoretical model of dissociation that provides a basis for understanding the major symptoms of trauma, and it explains how this model can be used in developing a general theory of the essential ingredients in trauma therapy. We'll also see how these ingredients relate specifically to the protocols of many of the somatically based trauma therapies.

8 KEYS TO
BRAIN–BODY BALANCE

YOUR AMAZING BRAIN, YOUR RESOURCEFUL BODY

When I was a medical student in the 1960s, we were taught that the brain was a complex but relatively stable and static organ. It was seen as being divided into regions that each performed a specific and genetically determined function, like vision or speech. Areas of the brain were often named after the scientists of the late 19th and early 20th centuries who discovered the specific function performed by each region. These discoveries were usually made by comparing the loss of a certain function, such as speech, with areas of gross brain damage on the autopsy or during neurosurgery on the brain. For example, Broca's area—which refers to the part of the left frontal lobe that determines the expression of speech—was named after the scientist who first documented damage in this area in patients who suffered from aphasia, the loss of the ability to speak.

There were few tests for "imaging" the brain in those days. Neurologists compensated for this by developing a detailed and complicated type of physical examination that included careful examination of sensation, coordination, strength, and reflexes. For example, problems identifying the vibration of a tuning fork on the great toe suggested something wrong with the spinal cord's conduction of messages, or something that was damaging the top of the opposite side of the brain where the foot was represented. This exam often took an hour to perform, but it gave physicians an inkling of the location of a damaged part of the central nervous system without having to see the brain itself.

During the mid-20th century, neurologists began to tinker with techniques that enabled them to examine the brain through X-ray images. These tests included injecting dye into the arteries of the brain to outline the arterial blood supply, dye into the spinal canal to outline the spinal cord, or air into the spinal canal to fill the fluid-filled chambers (called "ventricles") within the brain. These dramatic, painful, and risky tests did not show the brain itself; they merely demonstrated distortion of the position of the brain arteries or ventricles by space-occupying masses, or blockage of a brain artery itself.

These limitations in imaging the brain were swept aside in the late decades of the 20th century with the development of radical new techniques utilizing rapidly expanding computer technology. CAT scans, involving computerized analysis of X rays, and MRIs, utilizing massive magnets that cause vibration of protons within brain neurons and axons, allowed us to actually see specific lesions in the brain, such as tumors or strokes. And they showed not only the location of the lesion but also the specific dimensions and content, such as blood or tumor tissue. The field of neuroscience exploded, prompting the designation of the 1990s as the "decade of the brain."

We now can measure the size and dimensions of specific brain centers, as well as distinguish which brain area is operative and "on-line" with a specific brain activity. These tests depend on the fact that when we perform a task, the consumption of energy and the blood flow increase in the brain region we're using. For instance, with a type of functional MRI (fMRI), we can see the speech and vision areas of the brain "light up" with increased blood flow or glucose metabolism when a person reads a text aloud. We can observe growth of brain regions with enhanced learning and skill acquisition, and shrinkage with emotional illness and physical disease of the brain, such as Alzheimer's disease. We can also observe parts of the brain taking over function for other parts that have been damaged. In other words, using these new tests, we have discovered that the brain is plastic, resourceful, ever-changing, and resilient in the face of physical damage and mental or emotional illness. We have also found that the brain can, unfortunately, literally be injured, its function *physically* impaired as a result of negative life experiences, stress, and emotional trauma.

Understanding the Brain

For centuries, medical science has assumed that the brain, mind, and body occupy separate spheres in human function. The 18th-century philosopher Descartes noted that "the rational mind" and "spirit" are "separated from the affairs of the body." Medical science has in part adopted this concept as the basis for Western allopathic medicine. Although we have known for centuries that the brain relies on sensory messages from the body to organize complex behavior and acquire motor skills, we never realized that these messages were actively changing the brain in the process. And we certainly never considered that emotional experiences that were associated with sensory messages from a specific body region, such as pain in an injured extremity, could actually physically change that body part and cause a physical disease in addition to the injury, as in the case of reflex sympathetic dystrophy.

Today, medical science has set aside a whole category for physical complaints and illnesses that are believed to be caused by emotional distress. These are the so-called *psychosomatic disorders*. Often related to underlying emotional distress, they are not associated with any abnormalities on blood tests or imaging studies, and in the minds of many physicians, they are basically "psychological" or imaginary. The real dilemma, however, is that allopathic medicine relies on the measurement of "fixed states"—abnormalities that one can see on X rays or measure on a blood test—when the so-called psychosomatic disorders tend to be cyclical in nature, reflecting extremes of both the sympathetic, fight/flight autonomic state and the parasympathetic, rest/recuperation state. This makes them understandably hard to pin down with a time-based test.

A good example of a physical complaint caused by an emotional experience is that of disorders of intestinal-tract function We've known for a long time that the intestinal tract seems to be sensitive to emotional conflicts or what we call "stress." Television advertising frequently promotes medications for acid reflux disease (GERD), and irritable bowel syndrome (IBS), both recognized as stress-related conditions. We've now determined that these "emotional" gut disorders are actually associated with abnormal contraction of the gut and impaired sphincters (valves that separate different regions of the gut, such as the stomach and the esophagus). So, in fact, the gut in this case is abnormal: The brain is changing the body adversely in the face of conflict.

We've also accepted the metaphor of "gut feelings," sensing that perhaps some primitive instinct or form of knowledge resided in the organs of the abdominal cavity. And we've discovered that the intestines are packed with their own neurons, which actively send messages to the brain that may affect systems of consciousness and memory. Therefore, the body is having an impact on our state of consciousness, on the brain itself. These examples only begin to touch on the complexity of the brain-body interface.

The Brain-Body Dance

The brain, by definition, is an organ of infinite complexity and staggering dimensions. The number of *neurons*, the basic cell that controls all information processing, is in the range of *100 billion*. These neurons are connected to nearby neurons by dendrites, multiple tiny short wires. Neurons are connected to distant brain sites by *axons*, long wires insulated by a fatty substance called *myelin*. The number of dendrite and axon connections is in the range of *100 million billion*! And the organization of the brain is so complex that medical students routinely dread taking the test in neurophysiology.

The resilient body, through its complex systems of measuring messages from the environment, informs the brain of what's going on. It does so through signals from the primary sense organs of the head and neck, and from the skin, muscles, tendons, and ligaments of the somatic body. These messages from the body will alter the brain, as the intricate interplay between brain and body creates learned movements and skills for the body to carry out. The brain and body are involved in an elegant dance, ever changing and growing, developing body skills and promoting increasingly more complex neural connections.

On the flip side, stress and traumatic emotional experiences can alter the brain as well, injuring it and impairing its function. Stress and trauma do damage to the brain—damage that can be seen on an fMRI. Severe negative life experiences cause loss of neurons specifically in the memory centers of the brain. The infant who does not experience the closeness of the maternal-infant bond suffers shrinkage of a crucial area in the right front of the brain that provides regulation for the emotional brain and autonomic nervous system. The good news is that effective therapy in such individuals can not only improve and correct the symptoms but also promote physical healing of earlier damage to brain regions.

In my medical rehabilitation practice, I primarily saw patients who had lost function—physically, neurologically, and emotionally—as a result of injuries to their bodies, and often to their brains. Many suffered from both tangible physical injuries and the emotional consequences of that disability. I routinely made it my practice to educate my patients about the nuances of their disability. I believed that they were capable of understanding more about the functions of their brains and bodies than physicians usually assume. My explaining, in considerable detail, the brain and body functions that produced their often painful and frightening symptoms was remarkably empowering for my patients. And understanding these processes often helped patients achieve remarkable diminishment of their symptoms. Knowledge is indeed power.

My task in this book is to try to offer a coherent model of the brain—in all its plasticity, adaptability, and, yes, wonder—in a manner that is accessible to the lay reader. I'll review the anatomy and physiology of the brain and body in a way that most anyone can understand, and I'll also look at how stress and trauma can adversely affect both components. The Latin names for brain centers may feel like "Greek" to you, but hopefully they will sink in and give you a basic concept of how the brain works.

My hope is that you will be empowered by this knowledge and able to recognize yourself in the process, understanding how your brain and body "tick." I will try to tie together the intricate interweaving of the somatic (muscular, structural) and visceral (heart, gut) body with the complex functions of the brain in a way that will elicit some "aha!" moments, indicating you've recognized yourself. And I sincerely hope that you will come away with a message of resiliency and possibility for the healing of the brain/body in stress and trauma.

PART I

BRAIN–BODY BASICS: HOW WE FEEL AND HOW WE MOVE

BRAIN AND BODY MESSAGE SYSTEMS

It's a bit of a chicken-or-the-egg dilemma: Does the brain teach the body how to move, or do messages from the body train the brain in how movements are done? The answer is: It's both! I think of the brain and body as existing on a continuum—they each participate in the process of learning how to do something. The "thinking" brain may decide to do something, like toss a tennis ball into the air to serve it to an opponent. The act of tossing and hitting the ball sends messages from the body to the brain, which then adapts, learns, and changes its message to make the next serve more accurate. Soon we've got an ongoing feedback loop of the brain starting something, the body responding, the brain learning what happened and fine-tuning the signal, the body responding with increasing precision, the brain connections growing, and ultimately a skill emerging.

Let's say you're taking up golf as a sport. One way to start is at the driving range, trying to hit a little ball on a little cupped piece of wood with a 3-foot-long rod with a big flattened bulb on the end. The first few times you bring the club back and take a swing, you whiff the ball completely, or you hit the mat before the ball. Finally you nick the top of the ball, making it roll slowly off of the platform. Meanwhile, your brain is recording what you see, equating those visual cues with the feelings of combined muscle-contraction patterns in your arms, and is gradually moving the club head a little closer to the ball with each swing. Your brain is changing with each trial, signaling your muscles to combine in better ways to bring the head in contact with the ball. The brain is changing the muscular action, and the action is teaching the brain what to do. And both brain and body are changing inexorably and basically permanently. You are developing a motor skill through finely tuned trial and error.

This process goes on during most of our waking minutes and actually takes place during dream, or REM, sleep as well. It may be interrupted, of course, by injury, illness, great emotional distress, or trauma. But the healthy brain-body continuum is an ongoing, health-affirming process.

This brain-body relationship can also be broken down into somewhat separate systems, depending on the specific source and type of the sensory information and the regions of the brain that interpret it. Playing sports and playing musical instruments involve learning within different parts of the brain. Acquiring these skills can also be broken down by the different regions of the brain that govern gross movement and those that integrate that movement into complex learned patterns.

The Nervous System

The structure of the nervous system can be divided into two separate parts—the *peripheral nervous system (PNS)*, and the *central nervous system (CNS)*. The PNS consists of a complicated set of cells embedded in the tissues of the body. These cells are very specific in their ability to detect certain types of information from the environment. This PNS information may come from the primary senses of the head (vision, smell, etc.) or from the peripheral body (touch, pain, temperature, etc.). Messages from the head are sent to the primary centers for sensation in the brainstem, and messages from the body are sent to the spinal cord. Once the PNS messages are received, the brainstem or spinal cord will send them through pathways in the CNS that are specific for each kind of sensory message—in other words, each type of sensation has its own special pathway and center in the brain. These messages will then go to the areas in the sensory cortex of the brain that are specific for each type of sensory message, for processing, and for triggering a response.

The specific parts of the CNS are the *spinal cord*, the *brainstem*, the *cerebellum*, the *midbrain*, and the *cerebral hemispheres*. The spinal cord is a column of nerve pathways within the vertebrac of the spinal column. It receives sensory messages from the somatic organs of the body (muscles, joints, ligaments, skin, etc.) and relays them via a series of nerve connections (*synapses*) to higher brain centers.

The *brainstem*, or medulla and pons, is also called the reptilian brain, as it has changed very little from reptiles to mammals. It contains the nerve centers (nuclei) that receive the basic sensory messages of the prime senses of the head and neck (skin sensation, hearing, body balance, taste, etc.), and the motor centers that operate the corresponding muscles (face, tongue, throat, eye muscles, etc.). It also contains the pri-

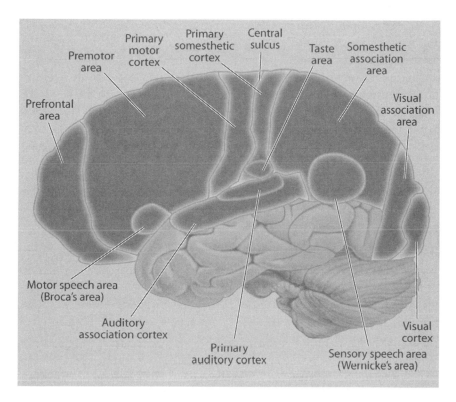

Figure 1.1 The Cerebral Cortex

mary motor and sensory centers that govern and regulate the viscera—the organs of the chest and abdominal cavity (heart, lungs, esophagus, stomach, small intestine, colon, etc.).

The *midbrain* contains a number of brain centers that, among other things, channel sensory and motor nerve messages to and from other areas of the brain, and help to coordinate patterns of movement and modulate pain. The *cerebellum*, as we'll soon see, is responsible for fine-tuning motor coordination of body muscles, along with the motor cortex and midbrain centers. The massive cerebral hemispheres contain the *cortex*, an outer wrapping that also surrounds the *limbic system*, or emotional brain. If you make a model of the brain by folding your thumb across your palm and covering it with your curled fingers, the fingers reflect the cortex, the thumb becomes the limbic system, and your wrist signifies the brainstem.

The cerebral cortex is extremely complex, governing all sensory message reception and all motor responses to these messages (see Figure 1.1). The most frontal parts of the cortex contain centers for the capacities unique to the human species that we sometimes call the *mind*—the capacity for insight, judgment, empathy, abstract thinking, planning, and creativity. The *limbic system* is the center for the modulation of arousal and emotional feeling and expression, as well as the center for interpersonal human connection and attunement. It also plays a large role in conscious and unconscious memory storage. Key 4 is devoted to the complex and fascinating functions of the *mammalian limbic brain*.

Sensory Messages and Motor Functions of the Head and Neck: Helping Us Orient, Identify Danger, and Communicate

Messages generated by the sensory organs of the head and neck—smell, vision, hearing, vestibular balance, and taste—are specifically related to our survival instincts and behavior. These sensory organs are conveniently close to the brain, and they represent the early warning system for setting off fight or flight behavior to guarantee survival. They interact closely with our emotional, or *limbic, mammalian* brain, and have many connections to the *amygdala*, a small, almond-shaped brain nucleus that is the danger alarm center and will play a large role in this book.

The head and neck are specifically designed to promote ready access to these sensory organs. Information from vision, smell, or hearing will set off the muscular *orienting response*, a rhythmic, side-to-side searching movement of the head that helps locate the source of danger or seek the presence of prey. The orienting response basically exposes all of the sense organs of the head to messages of danger from the environment, helped by the side-to-side exposure to these messages through turning the head.

The muscles of the head and neck—face, jaw, throat, middle ear, and sternomastoid neck muscles—are quite unique. Rather than developing from the spinal segmental muscles along the spinal column itself, they evolve from muscles in the *gill arches* of the early embryo. (Fish and early human embryos briefly have a lot in common: They both have gills.) Their sensory and motor primary centers are within the brainstem, whereas the corresponding centers for the muscles, joints, and skin of the body are in the spinal cord. Deriving from the gill arches, these muscles of the head and neck therefore represent an intimate and unique relationship with the primary senses, and are crucial for survival. And unlike the spinal muscles, they are directly run by areas of the motor cortex of the brain, and don't have to traverse the spinal cord.

Smells (olfaction), visual images, and sounds from the environment are the most important sensory messages that we access from the instinctual orienting response. The sense of smell is the most primitive, and perhaps the most vital, sense in this process. Animals, both predators and prey, rely more on smell for survival than on any other sense. For humans, the importance of smell in our survival has been downgraded as our species has evolved from the hunter-gatherer model in the wild to a primarily urban species. Nevertheless, the latent importance of smell is still reflected in many ways. The nerve pathways serving smell pass directly from the sense organs in our nasal sinuses to the amygdala, the early warning center for processing threatening information. So it's no surprise that those whose brains have been sensitized, most commonly by early childhood trauma, have a heightened sensitivity to minute exposure to smells. Examples are the development of exquisite sensitivity to odors, such as perfumes, old tobacco smoke, or recently installed carpets.

Vision, hearing, and vestibular balance senses also play an important role in survival behavior. Visual stimuli access the brain through each eye, with the image being focused by the lens and then processed in the visual sensory receptor in the back of the eye, the retina.

The facial muscles of the human species are one of its most important evolutionary achievements. We have by far the most individual facial muscles of any species, allowing for many complex expressions that give us an advantage. Facial expressions are intricately connected to our emotional, limbic brain, and they reflect our mood and emotional state. They are used unconsciously as a complex method of communication in the human species. Maternal-infant connection and bonding, and the social-emotional connection between members of the family and tribe, depend significantly on the appearance and expressions of our faces. As humans, we are literally programmed to talk with our faces. I'll get into the specifics of facial communication when I discuss the emotional brain.

Muscles of the face, the throat (or pharynx), the voice box (or larynx), and the tongue, of course, are the primary means of vocal communication. Although language seems to be unique to humans, most mammalian species also communicate with these organs. When the spoken word doesn't reflect the facial expression of another person, we immediately feel uncomfortable and suspicious. As we'll see, speech, language, and facial communication are uniquely sensitive to the effects of early life trauma, as was beautifully evoked in the Academy Award–winning film *The King's Speech*. The pronunciation of words, the inflections provided by the tongue, palate, and throat, and the pitch evoked by the vocal cords—combined with the complex interplay of the facial muscles—all contribute to our understanding of the message and the speaker's underlying emotional state. When any of these components are abnormally altered by disease, stroke, or emotional state, the message is partially corrupted.

Our sense of hearing is served by a remarkable series of physical and electrical structures. The eardrum, or tympanic membrane, lies about an inch inside the external ear, and it resonates much like a drum, with frequencies that depend on the frequency of the sound. In the middle ear, inside the drum, are three tiny linked bones, or ossicles, that pass the vibration on to the *cochlea*, or inner ear, where sensory receptors transfer the sound to the auditory nerve.

The auditory ossicles and tympanic membrane are respectively dampened by two tiny muscles, the *stapedius* and *tensor tympani*, which protect the system from damaging vibration from harmfully loud sounds. Some of you may remember how standing close to the speakers at a rock concert makes your ears ring. The noise has overwhelmed the capacity of the ear muscles to dampen the vibration, temporarily damaging cochlear (hearing) function. These muscles also contract to select for the sound frequencies of human voice inflections, or *prosody*. Prosody modulates and helps human-to-human vocal interaction, communication, and social bonding. So the stapedius and tensor tympani contribute to the emotional quality and meaning of speech. The tone and quality of speech sounds reflect the emotions of anger, sadness, joy, and love.

The vestibular system helps us with our balance. It's closely allied with the sense of hearing, both within the inner ear and at the location of their brainstem nerve centers. It occupies a site next to, and even shares fluid spaces with, the cochlea. The vestibular system consists of the *labyrinth*, three semicircular canals (half circles) that represent the three dimensions of space. They contain sensory receptor cells and tiny granules of calcium, which float in the canal and move about with movement of the head. When these granules hit against the sensory receptor cells of the labyrinth, the cells send a message to the brainstem vestibular nucleus, or center, which then tells the brain where the head is in space. The vestibular system therefore participates in the whole motor system of balance and coordination, and operates in conjunction with other specialized brain centers that organize complex movement patterns. When the vestibular system is disrupted, either by brainstem damage from a stroke or by damage to the labyrinth itself, the symptom produced is *vertigo*, an intense dizzy sensation with severe loss of balance. An intact vestibular system is therefore essential for coordinated posture and movement.

Sensory Messages from the Body: Telling Us What to Do and How to Move

The skin, muscles, joint capsules, tendons, and ligaments of the body all have sensory receptors, structures that provide the brain with information about the status of the somatic body. Some are sensitive to pain and temperature, others to pressure, stretching, and tension. Each type of sensory receptor has its own unique shape, structure, and function, and each sends messages that travel to the brain in separate pathways. All of these messages are sent to the corresponding part of the sensory cortex on the opposite side of the brain.

Stretch receptors in tendons of muscles set off the involuntary and unconscious deep-tendon reflexes (e.g., the knee jerk) that operate only at the spinal level. In this example, when the kneecap tendon is stretched by tapping it with a small hammer, the quadriceps thigh muscle immediately contracts, extending the leg. If the motor or sensory nerve supply to the quadriceps is impaired by injury or degeneration, the knee jerk may be diminished or absent. Similar stretch receptors in the joint ligaments and capsules send messages of *proprioception* to the brain, informing it about the motion and position of the joint, a message crucial for balance and coordinated movement. Tension receptors in the muscles tell the brain about the intensity of muscular contraction so that it can modulate that contraction for optimal function. When the sensory nerves of the lower extremities have been damaged by a neuropathy, one of the first things lost is balance and coordination. If you can't properly feel where your legs are, you have to rely on visual cues, which explains why people with a neuropathy have more difficulty standing and walking with their eyes closed or in the dark.

Exercise

In fact, it's more difficult to stand with your feet together and your eyes closed in general. Try a little experiment. Take off your shoes, stand on a rug, and put your feet together so that their sides are touching. Then do a few heel-to-toe steps. If you did fine, try this exercise again with your eyes closed. Then stand with your eyes closed and one foot in front of the other.

If you're over the age of 60, or have any neurological problems, do this cautiously by having a piece of furniture to catch. You will probably find that it's a little harder to stand with your feet together, especially with a narrow base with one foot in front of the other, without visual cues.

Pain and temperature receptors are present in every organ of the body, but in the somatic body they operate at the spinal level. That is, they send a message to the spinal cord that triggers a reflex muscular response that doesn't have to get processed through the brain first. A painful or very hot stimulus applied to the skin on a finger will initially trigger an unconscious withdrawal reflex of the arm. Pain messages travel from the injured part directly to the spinal cord, and then back to the muscles of that part of the body. This signal then triggers an unconscious, instantaneous withdrawal movement, even before you're a consciously aware of the pain. This *spinal reflex* promotes self-protective reflex behavior. When the message finally reaches the sensory cortex of the brain, you feel the pain, and the likely protective motor behavior, of course, is to put the burnt finger in your mouth, a conscious behavior.

All of these sensory messages—pain, touch, temperature, pressure, tension, stretch, proprioception—are sent along separate and unique pathways through the spinal cord and brainstem to the midbrain *thalamus*, the basic relay center for all messages, sensory and motor, to and from the cerebral cortex. Along the way, they cross over to the other side of the spinal cord or brainstem. There they are routed from the thalamus to the sensory cortex of the opposite side of the brain. The sensory cortex occupies the *parietal region* of the brain, which lies on top of other brain parts, behind the motor cortex and in front of the occipital, or visual, cortex (see Figure 1.1). Those sensory messages are then recorded in an area of the sensory cortex that corresponds to the area of the body where the sensation arose.

Both the sensory and motor regions of the brain are arranged in the cortex in a remarkably consistent pattern representing individual regions of the body, called the *homunculus* (see Figure 1.2). The homunculus overlies the sensory and motor "strips." These strips extend from the temporal lobe up over the cerebrum to the top, and then down the inside of the cerebrum. These body-representative patterns roughly place the face, head, and tongue down by the temporal lobe, the hand and thumb above it, and the torso and leg at the top, with the leg representation actually going down the strip within the fissure between the cerebral hemispheres. Our sophisticated tongue and speech muscles and our finger-opposing thumb are among the unique achievements of our

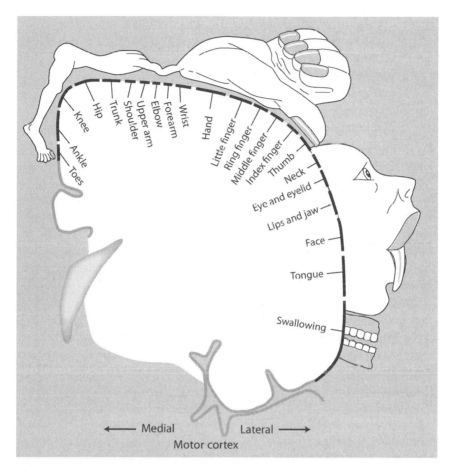

Figure 1.2 The Homunculus

human species, and they both get a large representation in the brain's map, with many neurons representing them.

The sensory cortex records all of these forms of sensation, and sends the information to the frontal motor region on the same side. The motor cortex organizes the sensory information and then incorporates a number of other brain centers to respond with an appropriate sequence of muscle activity *specifically responsive to the sensory input.* By itself, the motor cortex would create a very gross and simplistic movement pattern in muscles on the opposite side of the body. It needs the help of some other very complex brain centers to produce smooth, coordinated, and functional movements. Even putting one's burned finger in one's mouth requires a modest amount of skill and coordination.

Organizing Movement:
Balance, Coordination, and Grace

Again, patterns of movement that arise from the motor cortex are basically simplistic and gross. Fortunately the brain is very generous in its construction. Every brain function is supported by acres of brain pathways, bushels of ancillary neuronal centers, and an amazing intricacy of interconnections that support the capacity for ever more complex patterns of perception and movement. All one has to do is attend a ballet performance, a professional sporting event, or a symphony concert to be amazed at the refinement of movement that one can achieve by training the brain. This fine-tuning—this capacity for developing increasingly complex motor skills—is not just for pleasure and entertainment, although it helps with those, too. Rather, the goal of all brain functions is the basic survival of the species. That's how the brain is designed and structured.

Such skilled performance developed in the interest of survival relies on a highly complex system of spinal sensory messages interacting with brain motor systems, a process we've called "organization of movement." The neuronal centers are so complex that we still have not sorted out exactly how they work, what their evolved function is, and how they interact. Like the early brain researchers, we've learned much of what we do know from diseases and syndromes that impair function in these regions of the brain. We try to figure out the function they fulfill by looking at the deficits their damage produces, hardly a reliable presumption. So let's take a look as these centers of "coordination of movement," understanding that tomorrow the information may change dramatically.

After receiving the sensory information from the body, the motor cortex sends messages through the thalamus (the relay center) to a number of complex, and not completely well understood, brain centers. The first of these is the *basal ganglia* (see Figure 1.3), a series of small clusters of neurons concentrated deep in the white matter underneath the cerebral cortex. Their function is primarily *inhibitory*—that is, they put a brake on the gross motor messages coming from the motor cortex. For instance, tripping and falling is associated with an extension of your arm to catch yourself, a simple reflex act driven by the motor cortex. Jumping forward and catching yourself with your outstretched hand and arm as part of a gymnastics movement, on the other hand, requires fine-tuning the movement. This fine-tuning involves braking the gross motor message, which is the job of the basal ganglia.

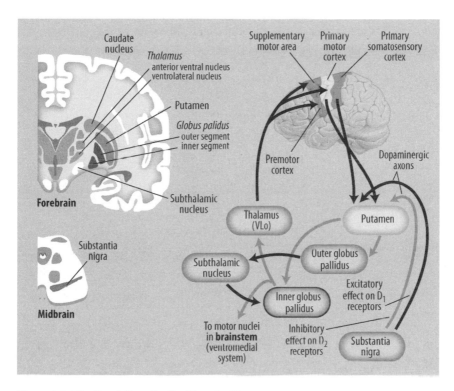

Figure 1.3 The Basal Ganglia: Braking the Cortex

From there it gets a little sticky, so bear with me. The *substantia nigra* is the most recognized center for control of movement, because degeneration of neurons in this small center causes the well-known Parkinson's disease. Parkinson's disease is characterized by a series of motor-control deficits. A rhythmic "pill-rolling" resting tremor of the hands is the most obvious, but not the most disabling, symptom. This tremor actually diminishes or disappears when reaching for something and resumes at rest. Another symptom, rigidity, is characterized by a ratcheting release of muscle tension (giving way in little jerks) when the limb is passively extended by the examiner. This rigidity is a reflection of the diffuse muscular stiffness in both flexion and extension of the limbs in this illness. The most disabling symptom, the impairment that is ultimately paralyzing, is the extreme and progressive inhibition of the *initiation* of an intentional movement, or bradykinesia (slowness of movement). Parkinson's patients have a unique difficulty getting up out of a chair, not because of weakness, but because the *initiation* of an intentional movement is so inhibited. If you test the actual strength of those muscles, they're fairly normal. The ultimate progression of Parkinson's is a patient literally frozen in place.

In the healthy state, the substantia nigra is intimately connected to the other basal ganglia, and functions to control head, eye, and body movements through *dopamine*, one of the brain's chemical messengers, or neurotransmitters. Because dopamine is diminished due to the death of neurons in the substantia nigra of Parkinson's patients, medications that mimic dopamine may partially, and unfortunately only temporarily, improve motor function. So one function of the substantia nigra appears to be fostering the initiation of movement patterns based on sensory input. (As you'll see, dopamine has some other paradoxical functions involving pleasure and reward systems of the brain.)

The other basal ganglia have long names (*putamen, caudate, globus pallidus*) and very complex functions. Their overall function, as noted, is inhibitory. They send messages via the thalamus to the motor cortex and put a "brake" on the gross patterns of movement generated there. For instance, if you want to sit down, your brain needs to put a brake on many extraneous movements, especially those that strive to maintain an upright posture. To initiate movement while standing, your brain has to put a brake on some postural muscles, and release the brake on voluntary movement. This fine-tuning of maintaining posture, initiating movement, and refining movement depends on the inhibiting function of the basal ganglia. So in injuries or diseases of the basal ganglia, one can expect problems with *too much* brake, like in Parkinson's, or *too little* brake, resulting in involuntary twitching movements like those seen in Huntington's chorea, a hereditary degeneration of the caudate and putamen.

Another brain center participating in the coordination of movement is the *cerebellum*, or "little brain." This structure, behind and below the back of the cerebral hemispheres, looks somewhat like a head of cauliflower. The cerebellum receives ascending messages of proprioception (movement signals) from the spinal sensory pathways related to sensory input from the joint capsules, ligaments, muscles, and tendons. It also receives messages from the *vestibular nuclei*, or balance centers of the brainstem and inner ear, which lie next to the cerebellum. Finally, it receives descending gross motor messages from the cerebral cortex via the thalamus. As you'll recall, the motor cortex responds to the original ascending sensory pathways from the spinal cord. Those messages that then descend from the motor cortex are seeking the regulation and fine-tuning of movements by the cerebellum (see Figure 1.4).

The various neuron centers in the cerebellum are specialized based

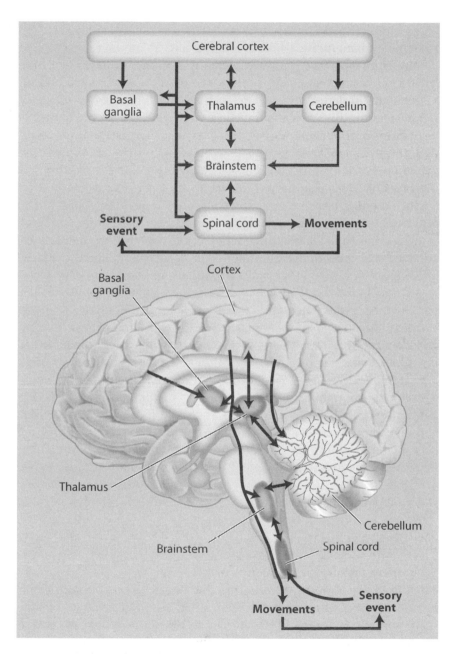

Figure 1.4 Note spinal messages to cortex, then to cerebellum

on the particular messages sent there: first, descending motor messages from the motor cortex, second, ascending sensory messages from spinal cord sensory pathways, and third, sensory balance messages from the adjacent brainstem vestibular centers (see Figure 1.4). The cerebellum puts all these messages together. In concert with the "braking" effects of the basal ganglia, the cerebellum then fine-tunes the gross motor patterns developed by the motor cortex. Through integration of this complex soup of neuronal input, the cerebellum acts to coordinate the whole package of sensory and motor messages, leading to smooth and integrated patterns of graceful movement.

In this process of integrating information from many parts of the sensorimotor systems of the brain, the cerebellum also is important for acquiring motor skills. It is crucial for learning how to do precise physical acts, such as walking, running, riding a bicycle, dancing, and so forth. These skills depend on an unconscious, implicit form of memory that we call *procedural memory*, and the cerebellum, along with the basal ganglia, plays a major role in this type of memory storage and skill learning. Procedural memory not only is the mechanism for acquiring and sustaining motor skills, but also is the memory system, linked to the limbic, or emotional, brain, which learns survival skills through classical conditioning. We tend to think of learning as a process of acquiring conscious information through study. But learning is also occurring continuously through the process of repetition of skilled motor tasks, and also through exposure to danger and risks. I will discuss this concept of conditioning, survival, and procedural memory in more detail in subsequent chapters.

The Two Cerebral Hemispheres: Speech/Logic/Insight versus Intuition/Spatial Perception/Orientation/Arousal

The two cerebral hemispheres in the human species represent the epitome of brain development. They appear as two quite separate knobby and corrugated loaves, sitting astride the cerebellum and brainstem (see Figure 1.5). The *cortex*, the wrinkled irregular surface, is actually infolded on itself in a pattern that is similar, but distinctive, from brain to brain. This infolding allows the massively expanded cortex of the human brain to fit into a reasonably sized skull. The cortex of a rat, by contrast, is quite smooth.

The infolded portions of the cortex are called *sulci*, and the knobby

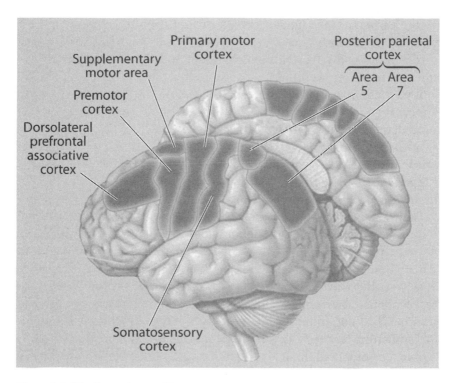

Figure 1.5 The Sensorimotor Cortex

ridges between them are called *gyri*. Some of these infolded areas are quite deep. Called *fissures*, these deep infolded areas separate different functional areas of the cerebrum. The major fissures separate each hemisphere into four lobes—frontal, temporal, parietal, and occipital. The frontal lobes, massively expanded in the human species, contain centers for speech, motor, and higher intellectual function in humans. The temporal lobes lying below the frontal lobes contain centers for speech reception, hearing, and memory. They also are closely linked to the emotional limbic centers of the brain, which lie underneath the cerebral hemispheres. (Recall the analogy of the human fist.) The parietal lobes lie behind the frontal lobes, separated by the large central fissure. Processing of sensory information takes place in the parietal lobes. This includes pain, touch, temperature, and proprioception—the primary senses of the body. The parietal lobes also process taste, sound, and other messages from the sensory organs of the head, except for vision, which is processed by the occipital cortex, behind the parietal region and at the back of the hemispheres. All of the primary brain centers are adjacent to *association* areas, which link the various primary areas and also store implicit motor, sensory, and visual memories for reference and comparison when new sensations are processed.

Each hemisphere basically controls the sensory and motor functions of the opposite side of the body, although small amounts of data are controlled by the same side. However, although the two hemispheres appear quite similar, their functions are separate and dissimilar. The left hemisphere is somewhat larger, and it processes messages somewhat faster than the right. The left frontal cortex, just above the temporal fissure, contains Broca's area, the area for speech production (see Figure 1.1). Numerical skills are processed in these regions of the left brain as well. In women, the left hemisphere is disproportionally larger than that in males, who not surprisingly have a much higher incidence of language-based disorders, such as stuttering, dyslexia, and language delays. The inferior left parietal lobe contains Wernicke's area, serving speech reception and comprehension. The rest of the left parietal lobe serves general somatic sensory information from the opposite side of the body. The most frontal (prefrontal) portion of the left hemisphere, the prefrontal cortex, is the seat of abstract thinking, insight, planning, intention, reasoning, and judgment—those functions most developed in humans. These functions are often attributed to the human mind. So basically, the left brain is *verbal, mathematical, explicit, cognitive, linear, intellectual, and logical.*

Patients who have suffered brain damage to the left hemisphere may have impairment of spoken expression of speech, comprehension of speech, or both. They may have impaired sensory perception of all or a few types on the opposite side of the body. They may have partial or complete paralysis, with tightness or spasticity (resistance to passive movement) of the opposite arm or leg, depending on what part of the large motor cortex homunculus is injured. Finally, they may have impaired vision in the right half of each eye, leading to right-sided *hemianopsia,* or half-blindness. They may also have problems with mathematics, logic, insight, and judgment.

The right cerebral hemisphere processes information more slowly. Creativity, dealing with novel situations, decoding patterns of sensory information and spatial relations, and processing music, art forms, and symbols are primarily right-hemisphere functions. The most frontal portions of the right cerebrum contain centers that regulate the "vegetative brain"—the hypothalamus and autonomic nervous system. They also facilitate social bonding and help to regulate the emotional brain, or limbic system. The right brain therefore is *intuitive, implicit, complex, affiliative, auditory, spatial, and creative.*

Patients with damage to the right cerebral hemisphere may have left-sided paralysis and spasticity, sensory loss, and loss of left vision. They also may exhibit other unusual problems with perception, not only of the left side, but of the whole body. They may show "denial," or the absence of perception that anything is wrong with their paralyzed left side. It seems as if their perception of "self" has been disrupted. They often have a "flattening" of emotions, or affect, with no apparent distress over their new disability, consistent with damage to the right arousal and empathic limbic brain. Unfortunately, they often have impairment of the capacity to enjoy positive experiences as well.

Although it is clear that the two cerebral hemispheres have many unique functions, it is a mistake to imply that someone is more "right brained" or "left brained." In fact, both hemispheres are "online" all of the time, and share information continuously. This process is achieved by a large band of nerve fibers connecting both halves of the brain. Called the *corpus callosum,* this band of nerve fibers overlies the limbic brain and transmits vast amounts of information between the two hemispheres at all times. There is evidence that females have a moderately larger corpus callosum than males, perhaps reflecting the slower intellectual maturation in male children. In addition, the corpus callosum is relatively poorly developed in infancy, and grows and matures throughout infancy and childhood. The growth of complex cognitive functioning in the latter half of primary school reflects this process.

Endnote

We've barely touched on the incredible intricacy and complexity of the pathways, centers, interconnections, and relative functions of the brain. However, I hope this chapter has helped you realize how vitally important the body and its sensory and motor functions are to the workings of the brain. Without the body, the brain cannot possibly fulfill its full functional potential, and without the brain, the body is useless. Each segment of this partnership is directly and intimately dependent on the others. Most importantly, the brain has the capacity to adapt and change, and change again, depending on the continuously evolving give-and-take of neuronal messages between both parts of the brain-body whole. This Key is the foundation for the concept of infinite interactive plasticity of both arms of the system—brain and body—which will emerge time and again in subsequent chapters.

ORGANIZING SENSATIONS AND MOVEMENT

We often take for granted the way our bodies function. Have you ever thought about how our fingers can learn the complex movement patterns for playing a musical instrument? How our brain can move our hands and fingers through the refined complexity of a Rachmaninoff concerto? How our legs and torsos can develop the incredible balance and agility needed to pull off a triple-axel maneuver in ice skating? How our body and arms can gain the capacity to throw a ball at over 90 mph through the tiny window of the strike zone in baseball? When a human baby is born, it basically has no truly intentional functional use of its body. The newborn is essentially a bundle of very primitive, instinctual, and automatic reflexes. It's well documented that the newborn infant, placed on its mother's belly, can crawl up to the breast in a very primitive fashion, and find and attach its mouth to the nipple. This rather complex reflex is actually seen in many other newborn mammals. In fact, most mammalian creatures born in the wild already have the instinctual motor skills to stand up and walk within minutes of their birth, a skill clearly necessary for survival in prey animals.

Although it is comparatively helpless, the human infant is born with a set of primitive reflexes that are the building blocks upon which all manner of skilled movements are constructed and learned. This learning occurs with the gradual development of the cerebral hemispheres, the parts of the upper brain that are small and underdeveloped at birth. As these regions develop, the corrugated ridges and valleys of the cortex grow in size and complexity. Expanding layers of nerve pathways begin to provide the complex structure that allows this motor learning to occur. As this process of growth and maturation occurs, the new, more complex patterns of movement suppress the primitive reflexes, which gradually disappear. However, if the well-developed adult cerebral hemispheres suffer injury or damage, the old, primitive reflexes of the newborn again emerge.

Postural Reflexes:
Foundations for Movement

As the fetus develops in the uterus, the primary centers of the brain mature and develop patterns of neural pathways that connect the reflex motor centers to each other. These early connections occur in the more primitive parts of the brain, the spinal cord, brainstem, midbrain, and cerebellum. They are identical in all human beings, although, like everything else, they develop faster in some fetuses than in others. But basically, all full-term infants are born with the same set of reflexes. Some of these reflexes involve the mouth and face and clearly are designed to help the infant and the mother in the process of finding the breast and beginning to nurse. Others are brought out by a sudden movement or loud noise, and are precursors of the adult startle response. These reflexes are the basis for survival behavior. Most of them have evolved to facilitate the upright posture that is required of humans to overcome the effect of gravity. So, along with a number of unique primitive reflexes, the brain is wired with a set of feeding, survival, and postural reflexes at birth. They persist for a number of months and then disappear as more skilled, voluntary movements emerge with growth and development of the cerebral cortex.

The *rooting reflex* can be produced by stroking or simply touching the infant's cheek or mouth. This will cause the infant to move its mouth in a searching arc, seeking the mother's breast. The *sucking reflex* is elicited by touching the roof of the infant's mouth, eliciting both a sucking and a milking movement from the tongue. This reflex allows the infant to nurse and gain nourishment immediately after birth. Also promoting nursing is the *snout reflex*, which involves wrinkling the nose and pursing the lips if the lips are tapped. These reflexes last a few weeks to a month or so, until feeding has been well established. The sucking reflex may persist for a long time, even if the bottle or breast is substituted with a pacifier.

Another series of infant reflexes are basically unconscious patterns that are the underpinnings of skilled movements that allow the adult to deal with the effects of gravity. The *palmer grasp reflex* occurs when the infant's palm is stroked with enough force to actually lift the infant, although it's only briefly sustained. The *stepping reflex* is produced by placing the infant's foot on a flat surface. The infant will extend that leg, and move the opposite leg forward, as if to walk. Similarly, if one holds the infant upright and touches the top of the foot to the top of a table, the infant will flex the leg and "step" onto the table surface.

The *swimming reflex* occurs if the infant is placed face down in water. The infant will begin rudimentary arm and leg swimming movements. In water births, infants have actually been observed to swim up to the surface after leaving the birth canal, and, like other mammals, to crawl up the mother's abdomen to the breast. The *tonic neck reflex* occurs when the infant is lying on its back. If the neck is rotated to one side, the opposite arm will flex and the arm on the same side will extend. This reflex is the primitive basis for adaptive balance. In the *Galant reflex*, if the infant is held belly-down and one side of the back is stroked, the back will flex toward that side. The *plantar* or *Babinski reflex* is produced by lightly scratching the sole of the infant's foot. The response will be extension (lifting up) of the great toe, and spreading of the small toes.

The *Moro reflex* is brought out by a loud noise, or if the infant is jerked or moved suddenly. The typical way to test it is to lay the infant on its back, raise it off the table slightly by its arms, and then release it. The infant will forcibly stretch out its arms, then fold them in and cry. The Moro reflex is basically the primitive precursor of the startle response in adults. The difference probably represents the early primitive posture of self-defense versus the more functional posture in the adult, and it may well represent the primitive act of attempting to grasp the mother. In the adult, the startle reflex is characterized by forward positioning of the head, opening the jaw, hunching of the shoulders, and flexing the thighs upwards against the abdomen. The adult startle posture suggests a reflex designed to protect those vital organs vulnerable to attack, the throat and abdomen.

All of these unusual reflex patterns are present at birth, and many serve a purpose based on the essentially helpless nature of the human infant. As noted, they are temporary, disappearing in the normal infant in 3 to 4 months based on the progressive development of the cerebral cortex. However, in the infant with brain damage or abnormal development of any sort—cerebral palsy, oxygen deficit at birth, a congenital anomaly of the nervous system—they may persist indefinitely. When they do, the growing child will clearly suffer from significant motor neurological problems, including spasticity or paralysis of the extremities.

These reflexes disappear with brain maturation in the healthy child because they are no longer needed due to the growth and development of the motor centers of the brain, especially those in the motor portion of the frontal cortex. However, as noted, these primitive signs and reflexes may reappear in adulthood if damage occurs to any of the upper motor nerve pathways. This reappearance implies that they actually are the underlying building blocks for the development of more complex cortical motor skills. Practice and procedural memory allow us to gain motor skills, but if there's any damage to the higher brain centers that control movement, the old primitive reflexes we are born with are allowed to emerge. There are many possible causes for reemergence of these primitive postural reflexes—strokes, tumors, traumatic brain injury, multiple sclerosis, infections or encephalitis, or degenerative diseases such as Alzheimer's disease, to name a few. If the neurologist finds some of these primitive reflexes in an adult on the neurological examination, it indicates the presence of damage to the more refined adult motor pathways. In this case the neurologist might order diagnostic tests, especially brain-imaging techniques such as CAT scans or MRIs. Even the most primitive feeding reflexes, such as the rooting and snouting reflexes, may return in adults with generalized brain diseases or injury, and are commonly seen in late Alzheimer's disease. So it is clear that they never go away, but rather are simply inhibited by the progressive growth of the motor centers that we depend on as adults.

Other primitive motor postures may also appear with damage to the central nervous system (brain or spinal cord). The human brain has evolved selectively for specific independent use of the arms and legs, as opposed to the four-legged walking or running in most species. Our legs are used more in the extended posture for running and standing, and our arms perform best with varied flexion and extension, with flexion being the most important posture. As upright creatures, we therefore depend on the extensor muscles of the legs to walk and run, whereas we rely on the flexor muscles of the arms to pick up, hold, and manipulate objects.

This basic reflex posture may literally emerge when the part of the motor cortex that controls the opposite arm and leg is damaged, such as in a stroke. The stroke victim typically experiences paralysis of the opposite arm and leg, with the extensor muscles of the leg and flexor muscles of the arm being tight, but stronger than the opposing muscle groups. As a result, the stroke victim may be able to walk, but with the leg in stiff extension, and the arm in flexion. The posture is called *decorticate rigidity*, and reflects the impairment of messages from the motor cortex that allow normal movement. The fine control of movements by the motor cortex has been lost, allowing the primitive postures of infancy to emerge.

Development of Motor Skills:
Learning Through Repetition

I've talked a great deal about the primitive and instinctual reflex "skills" that all infants are born with. Changing these to more functional, adult skills requires not only exposure, practice, and time, but also the basic maturation of parts of the motor cortex that will govern more adult skilled movement patterns. So the pace of acquiring motor skills is limited by growth and maturation of those parts of the brain that will drive them. But maturation alone does not guarantee that these skills will automatically develop. Intense and continuous interaction with the environment is the other essential key. Because adult caregivers by definition provide this environment, their continuous interaction with the infant is vital to this process.

The infant brain is designed to automatically copy the movement patterns of the parent. The infant will unconsciously bring its fist to its mouth and suck on it. When infants learn to grasp an object, it will of course go right to their mouths. If the infant grasps a rattle, and hears the sound, it will very quickly learn how to shake the rattle to reproduce the sound—and so on. What we see is an increasingly complex pattern of trial-and-error achievement of pleasure through manipulation of the environment. This fosters the further development of these increasingly pleasurable abilities. Infants learn by curiosity, intention, repetition, and reward. The pace of this process is dependent on the ongoing maturation of the brain. But the basic factor, the essential ingredient for this to occur, is the richness and varied nature of the environment provided to the infant. This process especially depends on the amount and complexity of the infant's engagement with the caregiver. There's a reason why newborn animals are so "cute." Kittens and puppies are basically irresistible. So are newborn human infants. When a baby looks backward over the seat of an airplane and grins at you, it's next to impossible not to grin back. The mammalian brain is designed to be entranced by their newborn progeny, and the infant's appearance is designed to ensure this mutual attraction. The smile of the mother when the infant vocalizes, gazes at a mobile above the crib, or reaches for an object is a powerful conditioning reward. Reward is very important in the process of learning skills, not only in infancy but also throughout life.

As the childhood brain matures, the capacity for more complex skills grows. All of these skills are acquired through the same process that occurs in the infant—curiosity, intention, repetition, and reward.

Reward systems become more complex, and they are based on the expanding interests of the growing child, praise from the parent, acknowledgment by peers, and so on. We see a two-step process—practice with gradual improvement, and then long, slow improvement even after intense practice has stopped. The brain continues to develop nerve pathways within the motor centers—probably especially in the basal ganglia and cerebellum—that enhance the skill even further without practice. The brain is consolidating the skill performance through unconscious implicit, or procedural, memory within these pathways.

The first part of this process, the initial practice with improvement, takes place in the motor cortex. With magneto-encephalography—recording brain processes with magnetic pulses—we can see that the motor cortex enlarges and its neurons fire more during the initial intensive practice phase. As the consolidation of skills proceeds, the basal ganglia take over and store the procedural memory for that skill, and the motor cortical centers shrink back to their baseline state. The learning process requires more neuronal activity in the motor cortex than the maintenance of skills does.

The process and the parts of the brain that are involved are basically the same, from learning to walk to playing a sport or dancing the tango. There are many psychological rewards in this process, from infant to adult, but it is of great interest that stimulation of the vestibular system, which by definition occurs with all movement patterns, has a very pleasurable and calming effect on the infant and even the adult brain. Pleasurable movements release endorphins, one of the neurotransmitters in the brain that produce rewards. There's a reason for "Rock-a-Bye Baby," the rocking cradle, and other methods of calming the baby through movement. Taking the agitated infant on a ride in a car is a great means of soothing. The same reward phenomenon applies to the pleasures of dance and other skilled movements in adults. We are designed to move, and the brain is designed to reward it.

The unfortunate flip side of this phenomenon in adults is that the *absence* of performing the repetitive skilled movements we've acquired through life causes the loss of those synapses and nerve connections in the motor centers that govern that performance. We continue to face the old problem of use-it-or-lose-it. On the good side, it's been well established that in aging, continued exercise *with our feet in contact with the ground* promotes not only muscle strength but also the balance and mobility associated with skilled movement. In fact, this kind of sustained motor activity slightly reduces the risk for Alzheimer's disease and may slow its progress.

The Role of Motor Memory: Unconscious/Implicit/Procedural Memory

Conscious memory, also called *explicit* or *declarative* memory, has to do with words, facts, and events. Although we use intention to pursue motor tasks, how well we do them primarily depends on the skills we've developed performing those tasks over the years. Some sports trainers use conscious visualization to perfect precise skills, such as "looking the oncoming ball into the racquet" in tennis, a teaching tool that tennis instructors use for novice players. But the tangible results of conscious techniques for gaining motor skills are quite limited. The secret of gaining fine motor skills is repetition while simultaneously measuring the success of the effort. The skill therefore is based on unconscious, implicit memory. Most fine motor skills would be impossible if one had to continue to "think" the movement patterns involved.

The most important form of implicit memory is procedural memory, one that I've previously referred to as facilitating the learning of motor tasks and skills. Procedural memory occurs with repetition of a motor act, and it is the primary way that infants and young children learn to stand, walk, run, and manipulate things with their hands. Recall the importance of the cerebellum in the storage of skilled procedural memories. Learning these skills requires no conscious intent beyond the initial physical effort. Rudimentary skills such as brushing your teeth, tying your shoes, or shaving are based on this memory mechanism. Once you learn these skills, you never forget how to do them, unless you suffer brain damage. The most highly skilled acts of motor performance are quite dependent on procedural memory, but they also may rely on more conscious intent during the initial period of learning. Even with prolonged neglect, the basics of thoroughly learned skills, such as riding a bike, dancing, or skiing, will always be remembered with reasonable effectiveness. Unfortunately, however, the brain loses some of its plasticity as we age. There's no question that the earlier one learns a skilled motor task, the more completely it's retained in procedural memory. As a skier who didn't begin the sport until my mid-twenties, I'm keenly aware of how skilled my children, who all started around the age of 6, are. Even if they haven't skied for several years, they quickly surpass me even though I've skied a great deal during that time. Athletes are basically built in childhood, as are musicians and others highly skilled in complex motor tasks.

How Procedural Memory Helps Us to Survive: Learning Through Classical Conditioning

If you've had children, you've probably taken delight in the pleasure they so obviously demonstrate as they mature and acquire motor skills. Human beings are born with the innate trait of curiosity. In fact, most mammals possess this trait to some extent. While watching squirrels or dogs at play, you can't deny that they're experiencing pleasure in this act of playful exploration. The canny designs of playthings for infants and children are based on this capacity for curiosity, exploration, and play. The earliest smiles and laughter of the infant are generally elicited by the mother's smiling face and the images of colorful and mobile objects. I'm sure that many toy manufacturers have a staff of behavioral science advisors who are well aware of the value of certain intrinsic rewards that depend on toy design. All of our basic senses, discussed in Key 1, participate in the process of learning through reward—and, for that matter, punishment. We may say that "curiosity killed the cat," but we can also say with equal certainty that curiosity *saved* the cat. And the same can be said of negative, or punishing, sensory experiences.

So the process goes like this: Curiosity leads to exploratory behavior, exploratory behavior leads to a sensory experience, positive sensory reward leads to learning and seeking behavior, and negative sensory punishment leads to learning and avoidance behavior. This is a rough template for the process of *classical conditioning*. And classical conditioning is based on acquiring unconscious procedural memory and learning.

The Russian scientist Ivan Pavlov (1849–1936) spent his long career studying this process of unconscious learning in animals, primarily dogs. He measured the responses of their body systems, especially salivation and stomach secretions, to a variety of external stimuli, including noises, electrical shocks, and visual images. These responses by definition were unconscious and unintentional. Pavlov found that he could create unconscious physical responses through both rewarding and punishing experiences, and that the connection of the response to reward or punishment persisted for a long time with just a few exposures. Of course, the most well known of these experiments involved ringing a bell every time the dog was fed. It took only a few exposures to this pairing before the dog began to salivate each time it heard the bell. The dog had "learned" that the sound of a bell was related to the reward of food. Pavlov went on to discover many nuances and layers of this learning process, as one might expect. What he discovered was the basic method of survival learning in many species.

Almost any sensory perception—smell, sight, taste, hearing, touch, pain, temperature, or visual size, shape, and texture—can be linked, or conditioned, to any other life event. It becomes what we call a *conditioned stimulus*. As I've said, the conditioned stimulus can be positive and rewarding, or negative and punishing. Either way, through this process we unconsciously learn about things to seek or avoid in our daily life, a very important process that helps us to survive from day to day. Conditioned stimuli all carry such survival implications. The conditioning event is often related to a negative sensory experience implying danger. For example, if someone has experienced food poisoning from a meal of fish, that person may permanently experience nausea with such a meal, and avoid fish for life. Getting stuck in an elevator may lead to persisting conditioned anxiety in enclosed spaces, or claustrophobia. On the other hand, positive survival skills are also conditioned through reward. Pavlov's dogs learned to value the ringing of the bell because it was linked to food. Parents' use of praise for good behavior is basically reward conditioning.

Conditioning of this sort is also dependent upon consolidating the behavior through repetition, or *reinforcement*. Without a certain amount of repetition, the learned response may fade or even disappear. Pavlov's dogs stopped salivating to the bell when it was rung a number of times without the feeding. This process is called *extinction*. However, many years later he found that salivating to a bell could be reinstated after only a few trials. One never totally "forgets" a conditioned response.

Extinction is much less likely to occur when the conditioned stimulus is negative or is a threat to life. Prey animals need to learn signs of danger—the predator—with one trial in order to survive. Pavlov noted the development of *experimental neurosis* in his dogs when he used repetitive negative stimuli, such as shocks or pain to train them to avoid the stimulus. Because his dogs lived in cages most of the time, they were by nature helpless participants in the experimental process. The combination of pain or life threat in the face of helplessness reproduced the conditions that inflict what we call trauma, and these dogs reflected much of the behavior we call PTSD. We will explore more about the brain and body in trauma in Keys 6 and 7.

Just because we live a relatively sheltered life as residents of organized, stable community structures doesn't mean that classical conditioning doesn't occur daily in our lives. Citizens of many third-world countries face tangible danger, often from other citizens, on a daily basis.

The hardships of extreme poverty, endemic illnesses, cultural violence, and civil conflict and war require rapid learning of defensive behavior through conditioned learning to survive. Although organized Western cultures and societies usually don't face these kinds of threats on a daily basis, they still are steeped in experiences that involve the process of classical conditioning.

With this in mind, we can begin to recognize that many of our day-to-day experiences and the behaviors that we display are related to this type of unconscious learning. The entire field of advertising reflects sometimes insidious means of conditioning our minds to crave certain things, from types of food and drink to clothing, electronic gadgets, automobiles, cosmetics, and so on. Reward systems, including appealing visual images, seductive sounds, words, and expressions, and stimulating music are designed to activate the pleasure centers in our brains and link the advertised item to a positive experience. Many employ humor, another strong positive reward. Many also employ rapid-fire image changes that often are much faster than our verbal brain is able to process but that our visual memory is able to store, relying on what we call subliminal information. We rely on verbal working memory to learn consciously. But we often find that we crave something without being able to give a verbal meaning to that craving—we've been conditioned by subliminal visual rewards.

I've proposed in the past that trauma tends to be inherent in top-down organizations in complex urbanized civilizations. The pyramidal, pecking-order structure of such organizations inhibits the capacity for those at the bottom to control their lives, creating helplessness. We tend to live in a cultural cage, just like Pavlov's dogs, and when we're faced with a threat, we tend to freeze and be traumatized. I call these traumas "little traumas." As a result, most of us have experienced some degree of life trauma, probably including the majority of you who are reading this book. In fact, the visual entertainment media has discovered that its audience seems to be especially attracted to images of violence. Those of us who have had some life trauma tend to generate the release of *endorphins*, the numbing, pain-modulating brain chemical, when we're exposed to violent or frightening visual images. Endorphins help us to survive life-threatening experiences. If the pain of an injury is suppressed, you can pursue a fight/flight response more successfully. Although such visual images may even be disgusting, we get a jolt of numbing due to release of endorphins, and even a "high" when we're exposed to them. That "high" acts as a reward, and sometimes lasts for a long time. We literally become conditioned to crave frightening images for paradoxical calming. It's no surprise that the top-rated television shows, movies, and computer games are related to crime, combat, or medical emergencies, with ever-more graphic images of horror. This social phenomenon may be an example of a harmful use of classical conditioning.

Endnote

The human species is the ultimate expression of complex development of the brain. Like a number of other species (primates, cats, dogs, marsupials, rodents, and tree-nesting birds), the newborn infant is quite helpless and possesses movement patterns that are mostly reflexive and nonfunctional. These movement patterns are based on instinctual reflexes residing in the brainstem and basic mammalian brain, similar to those in all mammals. Although by themselves they are rudimentary and not very functional, they represent the building blocks for the developing motor cortex to construct and fine-tune coordinated movement patterns. These complex movement patterns that define our uniquely human skills are acquired in part through systems of conscious memory and intention, but ultimately through repetition and unconscious procedural memory. Although we will never achieve the speed of the cheetah, the agility of the tree monkey, or the power of the lion, we can achieve skills in athletic and musical performance far beyond the capacity of any other species.

The human species also has much the same brain structure as other mammals for emotions, affiliation, and survival. Like other species, we rely on limbic neuronal centers to assess threat and to respond appropriately. We use the same systems of procedural memory for learning survival knowledge and skills. And finally, our brains use the same process of classical conditioning to learn how to survive. Somewhere along the way, however, we evolved a system of social organization that blunts the efficacy of continued healthy learning through everyday experience and conditioning. We will see in subsequent Keys how this plays out in the healthy autonomic nervous system, the emotional brain, and the body itself.

PART II

HOW OUR "UNCONSCIOUS" BRAIN RUNS THE SHOW

KEY 3

THE AUTONOMIC
NERVOUS SYSTEM

The autonomic nervous system (ANS) basically runs many of the unconscious processes that regulate the body. This system can be thought of as a physiological teeter-totter. When weighted in one direction, the body will go into a mobile, *sympathetic* state to respond to threat or pursue prey. When weighted in the other, the body will cycle into a resting, restoring, *parasympathetic* state, characterized by immobility and the storage of energy. This cycle of sympathetic and parasympathetic dominance continues throughout the day-night cycle depending on the varying needs of the body and brain.

The sympathetic nervous system prepares the body for physical activity and high energy expenditure. It dilates the bronchial tubes in the lungs to access more oxygen, and dilates the blood vessels in skeletal muscles and the heart, increasing blood flow to these organs. It increases the force of contraction in the heart and skeletal muscles. It enlarges the pupils of the eyes for optimum vision, increases the heart rate and blood pressure for maximal blood flow, and increases the rate and depth of breathing to obtain more oxygen. At the same time, it reduces smooth-muscle contraction and blood flow in the gut. All of this is designed to assist in maximal expenditure of energy for defense by the prey animal, or attack in the case of the predator, shunting blood flow from the gut and skin to the heart and skeletal muscles where it's needed.

The parasympathetic nervous system prepares the body for rest, recuperation, and the storage of energy. Blood flow and contraction of the heart and skeletal muscles diminish, and these muscles relax. Blood flow is shunted to the intestinal tract, glandular secretions increase, and the gut contracts to propel food and nutrients down its path for absorption. The parasympathetic nervous system basically supports digestion, storage of nutrients for energy, and sexual appetite.

The Fight/Flight Response:
Energy Expenditure and Survival

The fight/flight response is all about immediate survival, sometimes at the expense of long-term health. It's triggered by messages derived from the orienting response, and the early warning messages received through the sense organs of the head and neck (see Key 1). As you'll recall, the sense of smell is the most sensitive and important message system for land mammals that primarily function as prey. But visual, auditory, and vestibular sensations are also critical to survival. In situations of potential threat, these organs of sensation in the head become attuned to the threatening message via the side-to-side head and neck movements of the orienting response. This intimate mixture of sensory perceptions, instinctual body movements, and activity of the sympathetic nervous system operates to initiate the fight/flight response as a means of furthering survival in the face of threat, or capturing prey to satisfy hunger.

Most of the brain's alarm system takes place in the right half of the brain's limbic system. Messages related to threat or danger are detected by the sensory organs of the head and neck and are sent via a relay center, the thalamus, to the right *amygdala*, the alarm center of the limbic or emotional brain (see Figure 3.1). The amygdala then sends messages of danger to the *hippocampus*, a nearby memory center. These messages are then sent to the *orbitofrontal cortex* (OFC). The OFC is the primary center for regulation of the limbic system, or emotional brain, as well as the autonomic nervous system. The OFC is assisted in this function by another limbic center, the *anterior cingulate*, and also by the hippocampus, both of which contribute to keeping a lid on the amygdala if the threat is not significant. This servo-system of positive and negative feedback is an integral part of brain function. The OFC evaluates how serious the threat is, and based on that, tones down or inhibits further fight/flight behavior if the message from the amygdala is trivial. But if it's serious, the OFC activates the sympathetic nervous system response to the threat.

First, the right OFC will send messages to the motor cortex to start intense escape or defensive motor behavior. It will also send messages to the *hypothalamus* to initiate the hormonal response to the threat. The hypothalamus will send messages via the brainstem and sympathetic spinal network to the *adrenal glands* astride the kidneys, triggering the adrenal *medulla* to release adrenaline (epinephrine). Adrenaline is the hormone that produces the response in the body that I've described as dilatation (pupils, and arteries of the heart and muscles), con-

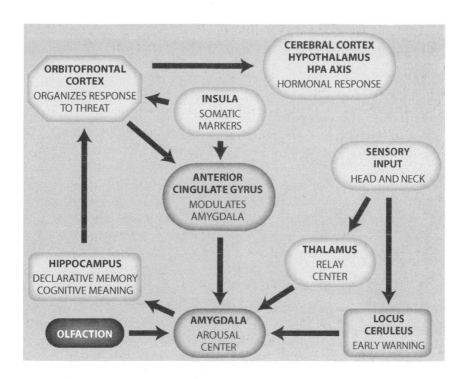

Figure 3.1 The Limbic Brain

traction (skeletal muscles and heart), and acceleration (pulse, blood pressure, respiration). These responses mobilize the body for intense physical effort. Finally, the hypothalamus will trigger release of ACTH (*adrenocorticotrophic hormone*) by the pituitary gland, via the hypothalamic/pituitary/adrenal axis (see Figure 3.2). ACTH will trigger the release of *cortisol*, the stress hormone, from the adrenal cortex. Cortisol helps prepare the body for the stress of danger if it is prolonged. Cortisol increases blood sugar, fluid volume, blood pressure, and vigilance. Both the adrenaline and cortisol pathways from the adrenal glands prepare the mammal for flight, self-defense, or both.

If the fight/flight response is successful, both the adrenaline and cortisol responses will subside, allowing the endocrine and autonomic nervous systems to return to their baseline resting state, or homeostasis. If an element of danger persists, however, the hypothalamus will continue to promote low-level increased release of cortisol by the adrenal cortex, which will continue to cause fluid retention, elevated blood pressure and sugar, and sustained vigilance. All of these processes help the body to adapt to low-intensity but persistent threat. Long-term cortisol expo-

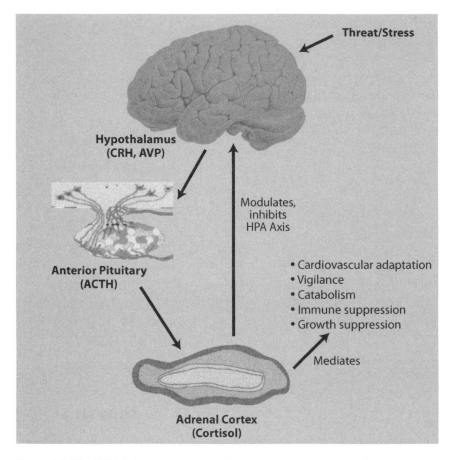

Figure 3.2 The HPA Axis

sure will also unfortunately promote elevated blood pressure, increase in body-fat stores, cholesterol deposits in arteries, elevated blood sugar, wasting of skeletal muscles, development of acne, and suppression of the immune system. This state of chronic stress potentially promotes the development of obesity, diabetes, coronary artery disease, and hypertension, the diseases of stress. If threat persists or is perceived to persist, systems begin to break down. Many of the patients whom I treated for whiplash injuries developed dramatic weight gain, acne, and increased facial-hair growth, or masculinization, during the first months after the accident, evidence for early and sustained increased cortisol levels. I'll discuss the negative effects of stress/cortisol on the body in Key 7.

In summary, the fight/flight response of the sympathetic nervous system has several discrete functions:

- Dilating the arteries of the heart, skeletal muscles, and lungs to provide increased blood flow and increased oxygen for increased activity
- Dilating bronchioles of the lungs for increased oxygen exchange
- Increasing heart rate and contractility for increased blood flow to skeletal muscles
- Dilating the pupils to improve the visual field, and relaxing the ciliary muscle that controls the ocular lens for increased distance vision
- Constricting arteries of the skin and intestines, which don't need to function in threat
- Constricting sphincters of the intestines and urinary bladder, and inhibiting muscular activity of the gut, which isn't necessary for survival
- Stimulating orgasm

The Vegetative Response: Procreation, Digestion, Rest, and Recuperation

The parasympathetic nervous system is less complex than its sympathetic counterpart, although new information suggests that it's more complex than we think. Its primary nerve centers are in the medulla (reptilian or hindbrain), and in the lowermost segments of the spinal cord. The nerve centers that serve parasympathetic function lie in the upper (dorsal) part of the medulla, the *dorsal vagal nucleus* (motor function) and the *nucleus tractus solitarius* (sensory function). The dorsal vagal nucleus via the vagus nerve sends motor messages to the viscera— the heart, lungs, bronchial tree, esophagus, stomach, liver, kidneys, small and large intestines, bladder, and sexual organs. These organs govern digestion, gland secretion, heart and lung function, excretion of wastes, and sexual function.

The cardiac functions of the dorsal vagal nucleus are quite primitive and simple. They basically evolved in reptiles to manage their relatively simple cardiac needs. These vagal motor influences on the heart put a brake on the heart rate in order to slow metabolic function so that the reptile could exist for long periods of time using very little energy and needing little oxygen. Reptiles are basically low energy-consuming creatures. In times of stress or rest, the dorsal vagal nucleus is able to slow the heart rate down to several beats per minute. This feature allows frogs to hibernate under the mud of a creek or lake for weeks or months without having to use oxygen, with a heart rate of only a few beats per minute. It also allows reptiles to dive underwater for long periods to escape a predator or to pursue a prey without breathing. The downside of this feature is that reptiles generally cannot pursue long periods of high metabolic activity. Like crocodiles, they tend to lie in wait for a prey animal, and attack suddenly. They are basically incapable of prolonged pursuit.

Sensory messages from the visceral organs travel back to the medulla via the tractus solitarius nerve. Recently, connections between the nucleus solitarius and the limbic, emotional brain have been documented. This relationship suggests that the gut may have functions related to memory consolidation and emotions, perhaps laying the foundation for what we call "gut feelings." The fact that very specific sensations, or "feelings," arising from the viscera seem to have a specific correlation with specific emotional states support this concept. After all, don't we call emotions "feelings"? And if you think about it, don't those physical sensations seem to come from the throat, neck, chest, and abdomen? We'll be looking at this relationship in more detail in Key 4.

In addition, the walls of the intestinal organs contain independent nerve cell clusters that clearly operate independently from the vagus nerve. These nerve centers in the gut use the same chemical messengers, or *neurotransmitters*, as the brain. Some researchers suggest that there is a separate enteric (gut) brain whose function is still not totally clear. Some have even called it the "second brain." We'll also be looking more closely at "the brain in the gut" in Key 4.

In summary, the vegetative response of the parasympathetic nervous system has a number of discrete functions:

- Constricting the bronchi of the lungs, increasing glandular secretions
- Slowing the heart rate, regulating heart rate with breathing cycles
- Constricting pupils of the eyes, contracting ciliary muscle of the ocular lens for accommodation and focus for near vision

- Dilating blood vessels of the intestines for absorption of nutrients
- Stimulating intestinal contractions, and releasing saliva and intestinal gland secretion for digestion
- Stimulating contraction of the colon for the excretion of solid wastes
- Stimulating contraction of the urinary bladder for excretion of liquid wastes
- Stimulating sexual arousal and erection of sexual organs for perpetuation of the species

The Freeze Response:
Last-Ditch Survival

Instinctually wired in the brain, the freeze response occurs when one experiences a state of helplessness while in danger. It is considered a "last-ditch" effort for survival. Those of you who have taken biology classes may recall that you were taught to "hypnotize" your frog for anatomic study by placing it on its back and stroking its belly. This simple act seemed to paralyze the unfortunate reptile so it could be studied without any interfering attempts to escape. What actually was happening, of course, was that the frog had entered a physiological state of suspended animation called the freeze, or immobility, response. This instinctual physical response is common to all species from reptiles to mammals, and seems to have distinct survival benefits. Because the frozen/paralyzed creature seems resistant to pain, some have invoked the concept of the freeze being a gift of evolution. But it also has some implications for survival.

In the mammalian species in the wild, predators attack prey animals not only because of hunger, but also because movement on the part of the prey instinctually triggers the predator's attack or pursuit. If pursuit of the prey by the predator is successful, and the prey is run to the ground and freezes, the predator may lose interest if it has recently eaten, sometimes allowing the prey to survive. Also, the female species of predator animals generally find prey to feed their young. If the prey "feigns death" through the freeze, the mother may then leave and fetch her young for the meal, occasionally allowing the prey to recover and escape.

We now know that both the flight and freeze behaviors are also associated with the release of large amounts of endorphins, the brain's pain-suppressing chemicals. If the animal were wounded in the pursuit, this analgesia would inhibit the need to move, thereby enhancing the animal's survival chances. As noted earlier, endorphins are also released in high amounts during the state of arousal that triggers the flight response. Soldiers wounded in battle have been documented to have increased pain tolerance for hours after their injuries. Once again, analgesia may allow the prey animal to continue fight or flight in the face of wounding.

Mammals have survived as a species primarily because of their capacity for speed and agility. The ability to pursue prey, or flee predators, requires a much higher capacity to burn calories and expend energy. It also requires a cardiovascular system that can pump increased amounts of blood to the heart and skeletal muscles to use that energy. So mammals have developed a complex system that can produce and tolerate extremely high heart rates. But every evolutionary advance also has a downside. In the case of mammals, that downside is a relative intolerance to very low heart rates and blood pressure. And the freeze response in mammals, as it is in reptiles, is associated with a marked drop in heart rate and blood pressure. Mammals don't tolerate that state very well. So the freeze response in mammals is basically a perilous state.

Many relatively simple studies have been done on the freeze response in mammals, most of them in rodents, especially rats. These studies show that naïve, or wild, rats have a high incidence of sudden death when they are forcibly immobilized by the gloved hand of the investigator, especially if their whiskers have been trimmed. Rats depend a great deal on their whiskers for sensory information, and their absence enhances the rats' state of helplessness. When those rats who died in the freeze are autopsied, their hearts are routinely found to have stopped in a dilated, relaxed condition, suggesting a profound dorsal vagal parasympathetic state typical of the freeze.

The early 19th-century physiologist Walter Cannon was fascinated by the concept of "voodoo" death in members of indigenous tribal populations. He noted that when the shaman, or "witch doctor," of a tribe pointed a sacred bone at a tribal member who had broken a tribal taboo, that member was thereafter shunned by the other members of the tribe. Such tribes thrive on a state of mutual attunement and bonding of tribal members. Such bonding, cohesiveness, and commitment to a common cause—pursuing mutual survival in a relatively hostile environment— are necessary for that tribe's well-being. As a result, indigenous tribes usually need rigid and sharply defined standards of behavior for survival, and breaking them is considered "taboo." Being banned or shunned for breaking such a taboo is tantamount to a sentence of death.

The "boned" member of the tribe therefore would often retire to his hut, compose himself, sink into a state of torpor, and die a "voodoo death." Clearly, this kind of shunning may precipitate a physiological freeze state, often fatal in the tribal member, as it was in the rats. The physiology of this freeze response is closely related to that of the emotion of shame, which may be triggered when a person is confronted about having engaged in an inappropriate social behavior, or "taboo." The physiological response to shame is *blushing*, a parasympathetic dilatation of facial blood vessels, with distant roots in the freeze.

But is this extreme freeze phenomenon and its fatal results restricted to indigenous tribes and witch doctors? Unfortunately, you and I possess the same brains as the unfortunate "boned" tribal member. Given the same circumstances, we have the same capacity to experience this fatal phenomenon. One of my medical school professors and mentors, psychiatrist George Engel, wrote an article on the study of a series of cases of sudden, unexplained death. What he found is that all of the individuals in the cases he studied were faced with inescapable conflict that couldn't be avoided or resolved by any specific means. All of their options presented them with totally unacceptable outcomes, a classic approach/avoidance conflict. They were all rendered helpless in the face of impending calamity. As the inexorable moment of decision approached, each one of them basically collapsed and died with no other apparent cause. They experienced the same physiological crisis as the wild rats and the tribal member subjected to "boning." The crisis was an extreme failure of homeostasis, with parasympathetic dorsal-vagal-initiated freeze and cardiac arrest.

Like other physiological states, the freeze response is not routinely fatal. In fact, it is rather common and can occur without the complete physical paralysis of the prey animal under attack, the wild rat immobilized by the gloved hand, or the tribal member suffering a "boning." The psychological phenomenon termed *dissociation* is a physical and emotional state that we experience or manifest when we've experienced a freeze response. We often refer to it as *shock*. For a moment, we're stunned, immobilized, numb, and confused. It only occurs when we've undergone a traumatic experience—one dangerous enough to be a threat to life or well-being—while being in a state of relative helplessness.

However, different people may have different perceptions of what constitutes a "life threat." A freeze/dissociation could occur with an episode of shame or humiliation, or upon learning of the injury or death of a loved one, or during an accident, assault, or other threat to life. It could occur when you get a letter from the IRS requesting a tax review, when you receive a notice of foreclosure on your home, when your spouse asks you for a divorce or a partner decides to end the relationship, or when you're notified that you're being fired or laid off. Although none of these events qualifies as an episode of "trauma" by the usual definitions, they all contain an element of a life threat. At the time of the event, you're likely to be helpless to solve the dilemma, at least momentarily. And that's enough to activate the dorsal vagal nucleus and set in motion the physiological events associated with the freeze response. You know that "sinking feeling" you get when you've received bad news? Neurologist Antonio Damasio uses the term "somatic markers" to describe those body sensations that represent feelings. That feeling is the gut's *somatic marker* for the impending freeze response triggered by facing a threat that's outside of your ability to control it.

It's likely that we face these types of freeze/dissociation experiences many times in our life. In fact, one nuisance that we all experience—the problem of "intrusive thoughts" or "mind chatter"—may have its roots in the freeze physiology. That recurrent worry about a financial problem or relationship conflict, that worry you seem to compulsively go over in your mind, contains many of the elements that cause the freeze and many of the features of the classic "approach/avoidance" conflict. In other words, they are usually associated with things that you really desire (approach), but that also have a conflicting downside (avoidance). These negative *and* positive features create a state of *helplessness*, the state required to trigger the freeze. I would suggest that when you're in that state of detachment filled with obsessive thinking about the conflict, you are actually in a state of dissociation, or the relative physiology of the freeze.

Now, we know that this is a very parasympathetic state, one that's likely to be associated with overactivity of those organs innervated by the dorsal vagal nucleus. These of course include the viscera—the heart, lungs, and organs of the intestinal tract. So what symptoms are you likely to experience under these circumstances? You'll probably experience, among other things, palpitations, heartburn, and bowel cramping, all symptoms of what we call "stress." If one extrapolates this phenomenon to our current human culture, it has many implications for health and disease, a topic I'll address in Keys 6 and 7.

Homeostasis: Cyclical Autonomic Balance, the Epitome of Health

The entire universe operates on the principle of the sine wave. If you've taken high-school trigonometry, you may remember that a sine wave is a smooth, repetitive oscillation cycling around a *mean*, which is a midpoint equally distant from the extreme of each oscillation. In other words, it is a consistent, rhythmic fluctuation of many things—the wave form in water when you throw a pebble into a lake, the rhythmic cycle of waves of the ocean and their crashing on the shore, the wave forms that create sounds and music, the cycles of the moon and the seasons, the monthly menstrual cycle, the daily cycle of levels of cortisol in our blood. One might call the sine wave the rhythm of the universe. These hormonal cycles of our bodies clearly are related to the physical cycles of our planet and universe, especially those involving day/night, light/darkness oscillations.

Our autonomic nervous system is subject to the same oscillations. Each state—fight-flight/freeze, exertion/rest, seeking food/digesting food, sympathetic/parasympathetic—is the opposite extreme of the other. Staying in one of these states too long negatively affects the body, causing significant distress and disease. Yet both states are absolutely essential for survival. They constitute the sinusoidal (related to the sine wave) form of the well-regulated autonomic nervous system. This state is called *homeostasis*—or, literally, "standing still." A more complete definition would be "*metabolic equilibrium* actively maintained by several complex biological mechanisms that operate via the ANS to offset disrupting changes." Because the sympathetic/parasympathetic cycles in homeostasis are constant and equal, we have a state of balance and equilibrium within metabolic processes, including the autonomic, endocrine (hormonal), and immune systems, all of which are intricately linked and responsive to the others. We're talking about balanced, rhythmic, cyclical equilibrium of many linked systems throughout the entire body when we invoke the term *homeostasis*.

The obvious question is: Where in the brain/body is the *generator* or master control center for homeostasis? Body processes don't just occur by themselves, in a vacuum. As you can see, this process of homeostasis is the quintessential element needed for health and survival. As with most functions in the brain, many centers contribute to each function of the body, and so it is with homeostasis. Perhaps the most basic and elemental region, the one most responsible for autonomic and endocrine control, is the *hypothalamus*. The hypothalamus is a small, complex brain center in the midline base of the brain, directly above the master endocrine gland, the pituitary. It has numerous functions, including control of body temperature, hunger, thirst, fatigue, sleep, and the sleep/wake cycle. One of its most important functions is stimulating the pituitary gland to release pre-hormones that trigger release of hormones from the endocrine glands—thyroid, parathyroid, adrenal cortex, ovaries, and testes. So the hypothalamus controls the endocrine system, which is the chemical manager of the body. It controls fluid volume to maintain circulation by balancing water intake and excretion by the kidneys. It controls uterine contraction and release of milk from the breasts as part of the birthing and nursing processes. It controls food intake through chemicals that govern hunger and satiety. It controls our metabolic rate—how rapidly we use the energy from the calories we consume. Finally, the hypothalamus controls the endocrine response to danger and threat through the hypothalamic-pituitary-adrenal axis (HPA) and the hormone cortisol, as discussed earlier. Optimal balance through all of these functions is necessary for homeostasis.

The hypothalamus responds to messages from both sympathetic and parasympathetic nerve fibers. It can perform its essential function by responding to signals from many sources—the ANS, the emotional limbic nerve centers, the frontal cortex, and even the reptilian brain. But it is the engine of homeostasis, not the driver. Given the opportunity, it will keep the body humming along smoothly and efficiently. But other regions of the brain play more subtle but important roles in this process, and enlist the regulating functions of the hypothalamus when needed.

So what parts of the brain enlist the hypothalamus to help with optimal regulation of all of these complex systems? Obviously, the emotional, limbic brain must play a part in this. This is the part of the brain that processes emotion and arousal. It's the part that's activated by and regulates messages implying a threat, and it triggers the fight/flight response when needed. Arousal like this, of course, is an immediate challenge to homeostasis. And the primary generator of arousal is our old friend the amygdala. If you'll recall, two structures in the right limbic brain act as modulators of the amygdala—the orbitofrontal cortex (OFC) and the cingulate cortex (along with some help from the insula—see Key 4). So activation of the right amygdala, and modulation of the resulting arousal by the right OFC and cingulate, represents one internal means of maintaining homeostasis. In fact, the OFC is thought by many neuroscientists to be a primary cortical regulator of autonomic function, and of the hypothalamus.

There's a growing body of literature regarding the practice of *mindfulness* as a means of maintaining a balanced emotional brain and healing trauma and emotional distress. Mindfulness, the basic state of perception that is achieved through the practice of meditation, is the opposite of mind chatter or intrusive thoughts. The goal in meditation is to "observe" thoughts as they arise, putting them sequentially aside while concentrating on the moment at hand—the treasured *present moment*. The breath is also a critical element in the meditation process. The process of observing the rhythmicity and depth of one's breathing in meditation is used to anchor this perceptual state of presence. This process involves several parts of the brain that play a significant part in maintaining homeostasis, which I believe is a critical role, and perhaps the primary goal, of meditation.

Imaging studies (fMRIs) of the brain during mindful meditation reveal that frontal regions of the *left* brain are activated ("light up") during this practice. The left frontal region of the brain under some circumstances is also thought to play a role in modulating activation of the right amygdala. This finding, although not totally conclusive, would suggest another brain region, and a means of activating it, that is involved in maintaining homeostasis. In addition, fMRI studies with mindful meditation show increase in the thickness of gray matter within the left hippocampus, cingulate, and cerebellum. One conclusion would be that meditation can physically increase brain pathways that govern focus, explicit memory, and modulation of arousal.

The breath work associated with mindful meditation raises a whole other issue in the search for sources of homeostasis. It has to do with the relationship between *heart rate* and *breathing*, and the brain regions and mechanisms that govern this process. The time-based relationship of our heart rate to our breathing is called "heart rate variability" (HRV). HRV is based on the fact that our heart rate optimally and routinely fluctuates with each inhalation and exhalation. In a healthy state, when we breathe in, our heart rate increases, and when we breathe out it decreases. This process basically occurs in all mammals. The relationship of this rhythmic shift in heart rate with inhalation/exhalation is a specific measure of homeostasis and emotional and physical well-being. The higher the difference, and therefore the HRV, the more optimal our homeostasis is and the healthier we are likely to be. (Please understand that this is a very simple explanation of this process, and many more complicated factors are present.) Low HRV is noted in trauma, PTSD, fibromyalgia, and many chronic disease states. After a myocardial infarction, low HRV is associated with a lower incidence of survival. In general, the higher the HRV is, the more one is in a state of homeostasis, and therefore optimal health. And there's evidence that the sustained practice of meditation may tend to increase HRV.

Exercise

This exercise is for people who do not already have a meditation practice. Find a comfortable chair, sit with your hands in your lap, and close your eyes. Do a body scan: Starting at the lowest point and working upward, explore any sensations arising in your feet, legs, and pelvis. Scan your abdomen for any tightness, cramping, or pressure. Especially note the region just below the end of the sternum, or breastbone. Note any tightness in your chest or throat. If you find any prominent sensation, focus on it, give it a name to describe the sensation, and note its unpleasantness if present. Take your pulse for 15 seconds, and then multiply by 4 to get your baseline pulse.

Then attend to your breathing. With your mouth closed, consciously inhale deeply but comfortably, and exhale for the same amount of time. If you like, you can inhale through your nose and exhale through your mouth. Try to attend to the quality of the breath, breathe deeply and consistently, and keep the duration of inhalation and exhalation fairly equal. Focus on the consistency and rhythm of the breath, and try to maintain continued focus on it. Do this for 5 to 10 minutes (it can be approximate), then breathe once more deeply, take your pulse, and repeat the body scan. Note any release of tightness, cramping, or pressure, especially in the abdomen, chest, and throat.

Many people have difficulty maintaining focus on the breath. Don't beat yourself up if this is the case. It takes practice. On the other hand, it's remarkable how one can notice striking changes in "feelings" in the body with only a few minutes of breath work. If you'd been attached to an EKG, you might even have found an improvement in your HRV.

Finally, a nerve center in the medulla, or reptilian brain, paradoxically plays a role in maintaining homeostasis. The neurophysiologist Steven Porges has proposed a theory, the Polyvagal Theory, that suggests that the heart is innervated not only by the dorsal (top) vagal nucleus that we've discussed, but also by fibers from another brainstem nucleus called the *nucleus ambiguus*, or *ventral* (bottom) vagus nucleus. The dorsal vagal nucleus lies near the top of the medulla; the ventral vagus nucleus more toward the bottom. The ventral vagal nucleus is present only in mammals, and also plays a role in regulating the heart rate. The ventral vagus "keeps a lid" on the heart rate in mammals so they don't "burn out" because of their need for speed and high energy expenditure. It acts as a regulator of the fight/flight response, inhibiting it until the prey mammal has a chance to assess the severity of the potential danger. But it also contributes greatly to an optimal, high HRV and therefore appears to be a player in the maintenance of optimal homeostasis.

The unique thing about the ventral vagal nucleus is that it is surrounded closely by the nerve centers for the muscles of the head and neck, including those that govern the *orienting response*, discussed in Key 1. The other muscles represented in that region include those for moving the face/facial expression, dampening excessive vibration of the eardrum, speaking or vocalizing, moving the jaws and tongue, and swallowing. All of these muscles are very different from other skeletal muscles. You will recall that they are all derived from the muscles of the *gill arches* from our early embryonic state, and they are innervated by the brain, not the spinal cord. The muscles that develop from them are quite special, and are critical for communication and for survival in general. Human animals have facial muscles that are by far the most complex and numerous of any species. The same applies to the muscles of our tongue, pharynx, and vocal cords. Providing facial expressions and oral communication, these muscles are critical in the process of connection and bonding between mothers and infants, members of the family and tribe, and the population in general. The muscles supporting hearing in the middle ear also participate in this process of mammalian connection. They dampen or release vibration of the ear drum, and select for sound frequencies specific to the human voice, a process called prosody. As I've noted, social, tribal, and maternal-infant bonding are critical factors in sustaining homeostasis. These critical nerve centers in mammals, located in the reptilian brainstem and allied with the ventral vagal complex, also appear to be essential to the maintenance of homeostasis through the process of communication and connection, and by modulating the cardiac response to threat. I'll revisit this topic in Key 4 when we look at Porges's Social Engagement System.

Endnote

The autonomic nervous system (ANS) is basically the engine that runs the body. It is responsive to many sources of information, influence, and direction from both the brain and the body based on ongoing experience. And it requires the complex interaction of input from many sources to keep running smoothly. Although it often operates at extremes of sympathetic and parasympathetic functional states, it is in a cyclical, ever-changing state that constantly attends to the needs of the body. These needs are determined by the range of one's moment-to-moment sensory experiences that relate to survival. And it is totally unconscious.

The ANS operates in a rhythmic, cyclical fashion. When that function is optimally stable, it is called "homeostasis." Although the processes that achieve homeostasis are mostly unconscious, one can consciously alter them and achieve the state of homeostasis through practices such as meditation and breath work.

As will be discussed in Key 4, the emotional, limbic brain plays a large part in the maintenance or disruption of homeostasis. And as we've seen, although the fight-flight/freeze responses, which represent the extremes of sympathetic and parasympathetic functioning, are intrinsic and necessary for survival, when corrupted by helplessness they have serious implications for emotional and physical health, and for survival.

THE EMOTIONAL BRAIN

As mammals evolved, they had to develop means to move swiftly about the land, in a variety of climates and changes in temperature. They needed to be able to hide from huge, predatory creatures including dinosaurs, which probably were relatively warm-blooded and very fast. They had to detect danger based on subtle cues, and respond instantly to threat, but be able to make quick decisions about the validity of the threat so as not to waste precious energy. With their high energy consumption, they could not afford to lay dozens of eggs in the hope that 10% might survive, as reptiles do. So they had to be able to have a small brood, and the capacity to nurture that brood until they could fend for themselves relatively well. And they had to instinctually provide that nursing and nurturing until the infant mammal could leave the den or nest.

Thus evolved the mammalian emotional, or limbic, brain. The limbic system is a brain center with an alarm system so fast and powerful that, when activated, it overrides all other brain activity. It also developed systems of memory that stored vast amounts of information from experiences that pertained to survival without having to bring any of it to consciousness. As noted in Key 2, body-based procedural memory holds the cues to survival from prior experiences. It promotes powerful sexual drives to ensure that mating occurs regularly in order for the mammal to survive while producing relatively small numbers of offspring. It generates instinctual drives to affiliate with others of one's kind in tribes, herds, flocks, gaggles, prides, and other mammalian/avian social-networking groups for group survival (Facebook not included). If you've ever raised cats, and observed their passive, accepting behavior of the antics of their kittens and their total devotion to their well-being, you have observed the powerful results of the evolution of the limbic brain. Fittingly, this part of the brain sits directly astride the reptilian brain and underneath the cerebral hemispheres. It modulates all of the still-present base reptilian instincts while using them for survival when needed, and it integrates unconscious mammalian instincts and survival skills with the conscious human cortex.

The Mammalian Brain:
Emotions and Affiliation

As implied, the limbic, mammalian brain—also called the "emotional" brain—evolved first in mammals. Reptiles are devoid of emotions, and one of the primary behaviors differentiating reptiles from mammals is the capacity for mutual affiliation and bonding. The maternal/infant bond in mammals is necessary for survival of the newborn mammal, which, unlike the reptile, faces a period of growth and development before it can survive alone. Reptile infants, who are born within an egg sack, possess many of the instincts and motor capacities needed to survive alone. In some reptiles, their first act of survival is escaping their cannibalistic mother.

The newborn mammal, by contrast, requires the intimate attention of its mother for feeding and physical protection until the infant has matured enough to live alone. The limbic, emotional brain is already prepared for the mother and newborn to be instinctually bonded. This bonding process also extends to other members of the tribe, or mammalian species group, ensuring the survival of the community as well. The brain basis for this instinctual affiliation capacity lies in the limbic brain, which also contains neuronal centers serving the survival instinct, memory, emotions, and pathways for the sense of smell (recall the importance of smell for survival). Most of these survival/emotional centers are predominantly within the *right-sided* limbic brain. They are also closely allied with other neuronal centers within the temporal lobe, especially those dealing with memory.

Many people, including neuroscience researchers, believe that the mammalian brain is a leftover from lower mammals, and that the frontal cortex of the brain is the new power broker, accounting for the evolutionary ascendance of the human species. The whole concept of the "triune brain," or "three brains in one"—reptilian, mammalian, and neocortical, or primate—was developed in the 1960s by neuroscientist Paul MacLean. As you've seen, I've been using his model more or less throughout this book. But research over the past 40 years has proven that this precise three-part division of anatomy and function based on evolution of the species is much more complex than what McLean proposed. There is clear evidence that much of the behavior that we consider to be unique to primates, and especially humans, is also present in "lesser" species. These traits include perception, memory and the capacity to learn, the use of language, the use of tools, and the selective nurturing of infants. Many of these traits are present in subhuman primates, and in fact in other mammals and birds. Birds communicate through a complex pattern of calls, and have complex social systems. Many species mate for life, and all are totally devoted to the care of their young. Some have the capacity for mimicry, including of human speech. The lines separating the divisions of the triune brain are clearly quite blurred. But for our purposes, I will continue to refer to the emotional/limbic brain when I address emotions and survival.

The human neocortex does provide unique functions such as formal language, insight, planning, and abstract thinking. Still, there is increasing recognition that the emotional, limbic brain may influence, and even dominate, what we consider to be rational thinking and intelligence, and may have more to do with the way we think and make decisions than our vaunted neocortex does. Theoretically, if we recognize that emotions play a large role in how we think or express our intelligence, then we perhaps could use our intelligence to control our emotions.

The recognition of the role of intelligence in managing emotions has given rise to the complex concept of *emotional intelligence* (EI). This concept basically involves the ability to be aware of and manage one's own emotions, as well as those of other people, on a social and relational level. These skills are based, therefore, on insight and empathy, a blending of the intellect and the emotions. Extreme disability in this skill is called *alexithymia*, which refers to being relatively unable, or even completely unable, to understand, process, or describe one's own emotions. Alexithymia is seen in a number of mental disorders, including late PTSD, or complex trauma, and Axis II personality disorders such as borderline personality disorder, with self-mutilation.

EI has been criticized as being an artificial concept that is difficult to measure or prove. It involves so many diverse states linking emotions to intellectual function that "standardized tests" for EI have been relatively inconclusive. The concept does, however, illustrate the vexing role of emotions in the way we apply logic to a situation, why we keep repeating dysfunctional patterns in relationships, and why our supposedly intelligent choices don't make sense or are self-defeating. It also is a measure of how our brains perform in stress and trauma (addressed further in Key 6).

I've discussed the parts of the emotional brain that are related to empathy and maternal-infant and societal attunement and bonding—namely the anterior cingulate cortex, the insula, and the orbitofrontal cortex. In humans, these areas have been documented to be activated when we feel emotions, and also when we observe emotions being experienced by other people. In fact, people who test strongly for the capacity for empathy on standardized questionnaires are shown to test highly for mirror neurons in brain centers serving EI.

Sensory Messages from the Gut: Telling Us How We Feel

"I just know it must be true—I can feel it in my gut!" How often have we heard that heartfelt (or gut-felt) assertion? In fact, our social vernacular clearly equates the concept of "feelings" with emotion. And if you stop and think about it, our emotions really do seem to have a body sensation associated with them. Panic and anxiety are often experienced as a "sinking feeling in the stomach," usually a point in the upper abdomen just below the sternum. Joy, love, and ecstasy often are associated with a feeling of warmth and expansion in the upper chest and throat. Anger and rage relate to a sensation of tightness in the chest and abdomen, shame with a hot sensation (and blush!) in the face, grief with heaviness in the chest, terror with a choking feeling in the throat and cramping in the lower "gut," and so on.

These very real sensations arise from the *viscera*, or organs of the chest and abdominal cavities. They include the lungs, especially the bronchial tubes, the larynx (voice box) and pharynx (throat), the heart, the stomach, and the small and large intestines. If you were to test the function of these organs at the time of the presence of emotional "feelings," you would find that the muscle contractions of these organs, and the arterial blood supply, are actually altered by the emotion, creating the classic sensations I just described. "Feelings" have a physical cause. All of these vegetative, visceral organs have receptors for pain and for detecting stretching or contraction of their smooth muscles, just like the somatic striated muscles of your body. These "feelings" actually have more to do with the intensity and validity of our emotional state than their accompanying thought processes do. So is the physical sensation or the emotional thought the basic element of the emotion? Clearly they are inseparable, and perhaps equal. But I would maintain that without the "gut feeling," the emotion's significance would be profoundly impaired.

You'll recall that neurologist Antonio Damasio emphasized the role of "feelings" in our intrinsic self-perception and called these feelings *somatic markers*. He noted that feelings accompany almost any significant life experience and are with us constantly. Their role is to inform our conscious and unconscious emotional brains about our state of well- or ill-being in the moment, and to create a subtext of meaning for that moment and for our ongoing life in general. Our somatic markers identify the emotional meaning of the present moment. Although the most potent source of self-information with feelings arises from the viscera, the somatic, external muscular body also has a role in providing "feelings" that represent our emotional self. These feelings are usually related to tightness or stiffness felt in muscles, as well as tingling, numbness, flushing, or coldness felt in the skin. They reflect the status of the *autonomic nervous* system and its control of circulation to those muscles and their state of contraction, as well as circulation to the skin. Actual pain felt in the somatic body may represent old traumatic procedural memories brought to consciousness by a current cue to an old threatening experience. Somatic "feelings" often tend to reflect emotions related to danger, arousal, and the need for self-protection, which would recruit the muscles of the body for fight or flight.

Exercise

Put down the book, and sit in a comfortable chair. Find a comfortable posture, place your hands in your lap, and shut your eyes. Now, scan through your recollections for any unresolved conflict, danger, loss, or other recent negative life experience. Congratulations if you have difficulty coming up with one. If you can't think of anything, you can go back to similar past events, even those that seem to have been resolved. Concentrate on the event, especially its most painful aspects. Think of the person involved and the words that may have been exchanged. If the experience was not personal, analyze its specific nature and the emotions you may have experienced. After 5 minutes or so, scan your body for any prominent "feelings," beginning with your feet and then progressing up your legs, pelvis, and torso, emphasizing the abdomen, chest, and throat. Note whatever sensations seem to be prominent, and whether they are unpleasant. If you find this exercise distressing, stop, take four or five deep, cleansing breaths, and open your eyes. Note any residual sensations and emotions.

The other major consideration is the inescapable fact that, in a negative emotion, not only does the "feeling" accompany and reflect the emotion, but the visceral organ for that moment is also functionally changed. In other words, the organ's normal, life-serving function, such as digesting food, has been temporarily interrupted or altered. This is not a very functional state of affairs. It seems that vehement emotions are not just unpleasant, but perhaps even harmful. And the region that will probably take the brunt of the vehement emotion is the viscera. This opens up a whole new can of worms—the dubious and often disparaged concept of psycho- (emotional) somatic (physical) disease. The extremes of emotional feeling states are associated with the physical feelings/symptoms of conditions that are thought to be just "in your head" by many physicians. But, in fact, they are the inevitable result of states of high emotions. They are a message to which we need to pay attention. This concept of the mind-body interface on the precipice of disease is addressed in Key 7.

Memory and Survival:
The Amygdala, Hippocampus, and
Some Fellow Travelers

The primary neuronal center for survival, as you'll recall, is the *amygdala*, which lies in the temporal lobe part of the limbic system (see Figure 3.1). This important center is the first to receive sensory messages of threat or danger, and it is basically the center for arousal or fear. Its primary function is to set off the fight/flight response for the purpose of survival. It also contributes to storing survival-based memories and plays an active role in producing the symptoms of PTSD, or traumatic stress, when its function has been corrupted in trauma.

The amygdala has numerous and rich neuronal connections with all of the other limbic centers, and it plays a large role in storing long-term memories that are based on a threatening experience and have implications for survival. The downside of this, of course, is that such emotional memories linked to unresolved, negative, or traumatic events and emotions tend to be intrusive. They keep recurring with other memory cues for the trauma, and they actually corrupt our attempts at conscious awareness and concentration. As we'll see, this process is the substance of trauma. However, powerful memories linked to positive experiences also tend to be stored accurately and permanently by the amygdala. We often call these types of memories our *autobiographical* memories, memories from important life events. Powerful positive memories also have survival implications as a template for the benchmarks of our lives.

Just behind the amygdala in the temporal lobe lies the *hippocam-*

pus, a larger structure whose role is the storage of conscious, explicit, or *declarative* memories having to do with learning and remembering facts and events. Whatever you remember from reading this book will have been partially stored in your hippocampus. The hippocampus is an older part of the limbic system and is linked spatially to other parts of the brain that relate to the nature of the sensory information of the memory. It's active when you try to find your car in the parking lot at the mall or find your way around a new town. Short-term, working memory is processed there. Memory is duplicated in the hippocampus on both sides, and it takes destruction of both of them to destroy short-term memory. It is also one of the most plastic centers of the brain, both with regard to enlargement with training and shrinkage with stress and trauma. There are a number of important subtypes of explicit, declarative memory.

Short-term, or *working*, memory is in a class all its own. We use it to remember information about things that are happening to us from moment to moment, and to sort out the important information and reject the irrelevant. For example, watching a movie or having a conversation requires us to store what we've seen or heard for a period of up to about 5 to 10 seconds in order to relate it to what happens next. Our coherent experience as we pass through time requires this brief *working* memory to form a template, or background, for what happens next. Otherwise nothing in the passage of our lives would make sense.

Transient global amnesia is an interesting, even bizarre syndrome that is characterized by the sudden onset of complete but temporary loss of short-term, working memory. Individuals struck with this disorder suddenly are unable to remember anything that goes on longer than 2 to 3 seconds. They typically will ask the same question over and over, never actually storing the answer in working memory. They usually will appear confused but otherwise normal. They will know familiar people around them, and even events from their past, but for a variable period from a few minutes to a few hours, every moment is new and disconnected from the previous one. The deficit will rather suddenly end, and usually after a few minutes or hours the short-term memory will completely return. But the patient will never have a conscious memory for events during that bizarre interlude. The syndrome is benign, the cause unknown, and from case to case it always behaves in virtually the same manner.

As we age, the effectiveness of short-term memory will decline, even in the healthy individual. This decline is variable, but inevitable enough for us to call this apparent attention deficit a "senior moment." Occasionally it may be the precursor to Alzheimer's disease. In fact, new studies show that sustained, regular exercise and "new" learning (not Sudoku or crossword puzzles) may be the most important activity to prevent or slow the normal decline in working memory and attention that we see with aging, and may actually mitigate the development of Alzheimer's disease.

I've already referred to concepts of "explicit" versus "implicit" memory. Both of these fall under the category of *long-term* memory. A long-term memory is anything that you still recall after a few minutes. Depending on the importance of this memory, it may last for days to years, or become permanent. The importance may be determined by motivation, intentional attempts to learn, and the emotional content of the memory. One can enhance long-term memory through elaborate training methods leading to such phenomena as the entertaining "Zip Code Man," an individual who laboriously trained his long-term memory to store the location of every zip code in the United States. Although usually fairly hard-wired, long-term memories can be altered by other, newer memories with similar content. Long-term memories are stored in many and varied areas of the brain based on their content. Long-term memory is actually what we call "learning," and we use it throughout our education to acquire the knowledge necessary for our budding careers. Such long-term memory requires repeated consolidation and reinforcement through frequent retrieval in order for it to remain useful. You either use it or you lose it. I often say that I probably remember only about 10% of what I learned in medical school. What I *have* recalled are medical facts that I've used over and over again in the context of practicing medicine.

Explicit memory, as I've noted, is also called "declarative memory," implying that it's involved with words. It has to do with the storage of facts and events—what one does when trying to remember what's being taught in class, or in this case what one has just read, and wants to remember for further reference. It's the part of memory that we use to store information for future use—or *learn*. You're using it right now as you read this, hoping to learn new information. Explicit memory also is dependent on associations—your brain links related explicit memories together to form a matrix of related concepts in your life. So when you think of the house where you grew up, you automatically remember your parents and siblings, the neighborhood, the school you went to, your playmates, and so on. Linking many declarative memories together is a way of consolidating all of them. Retention of declarative memories is also enhanced by any positive or negative emotion related to them.

Learning words, concepts, and other verbal material is a subset of explicit memory called *semantic* memory. Semantic memory is acquired in childhood. It's basically our general knowledge about the world, such as the names of animals, family members, common geography, and basic life facts, and it is often learned through our parents, elementary school, books we've read, and stories we've been told as children. This type of semantic memory is relatively permanent. We also use this type of memory to learn a profession or a mental skill. Some call it *textbook learning.* Hopefully semantic memory learned through study sticks around for a long time, because our mental and intellectual skills depend on it, as may our livelihood. But its permanence depends on repetitive use in our daily life. It will fade if it's not called to consciousness fairly regularly. Semantic memory is probably stored primarily in the hippocampus, although <u>much</u> of it is probably also stored in other parts of the cerebral cortex that reflect the content of the memory.

A second type of explicit memory is *episodic* memory. Episodic memory, as the word implies, is about personal life events, or episodes. It therefore is autobiographical. Much of this type of memory is very transient and easily forgotten. But other parts, usually those that are associated with any emotional content that has special meaning to us, are relatively hard-wired. Linking an emotion to a life experience creates a meaning for survival that renders its memory quite permanent. Such a memory will often contain elements of body-based memories. In my lectures, I offer an example by asking the audience what comes to mind when they remember first seeing the plane hit the tower on September 11, 2001. The visual image on the television usually comes to mind, and it often is linked to related sensory experiences, such as the smell of fresh-brewed coffee because the attack occurred in the morning. Other emotion-linked life memories, such as special family events—marriages, deaths, athletic successes, and so on—assume the state of permanent episodic memories. These memories are primarily stored in the hippocampus, but also in areas of the cortex related to the sensorimotor content of the memory. When the emotional association is very intense, and therefore linked to survival, this type of episodic memory can be considered *implicit*, or permanent.

Memory is an important function of the emotional brain, both for the purposes of learning and for survival through the functions of the amygdala. Because it deals with emotion, it particularly relies on a system of checks and balances in order to function. We would certainly burn out in a hurry, both physically and emotionally, if there weren't built-in regulating systems, or governors that serve to modulate and control arousal and other vehement emotions. The right emotional brain therefore contains a system of interactive brain centers that provides this series of checks and balances. Not surprisingly, these modulating brain centers are also closely related to attachment, attunement, communication, and social engagement.

Emotional Modulation:
The Anterior Cingulate, the Insula, the OFC,
and the Ventral Vagus

The first of these modulating brain centers is the *anterior cingulate cortex*, or *gyrus*, an upper limbic cortical structure (see Figure 3.1 on page 41). The anterior cingulate cortex has a number of functions, including inhibiting or regulating the amygdala and regulating the autonomic nervous system and emotions in general to promote balance. It also inhibits impulsivity, promotes attention and learning, and helps with emotional control. Further functions include sustaining the state of consciousness and supporting empathy and affiliation. Along with the orbitofrontal cortex (OFC) and insula, it is an agent for sustaining homeostasis.

The *insula*, or *insular cortex*, is a portion of the cerebral cortex that is frequently included in the emotional brain. It's located deep beneath the frontal and temporal lobes, under the temporal fissure. Neurologist Antonio Damasio describes the function of the insula as storing conscious *feelings*. These feelings reflect visceral (gut) and skeletal (somatic body) states, and their sensations, which in turn are associated with emotions. Recall that the insula basically provides a map of the emotional brain in the moment through what Damasio calls *somatic markers*. These parts of the *felt sense* are the body's representation of our state of well-being through sensations, or feeling states.

Such sensations are extremely important in informing the brain about the state of well-being of the body and the self, and therefore the state of consciousness. These feelings tell us whether we are frightened, aroused, excited, disgusted, grief-stricken, ecstatic, depressed, or any other state of increased emotion. We usually don't even think about the body state we're feeling—we only tend to sense its corresponding emotion. Each emotion not only has a *visceral* sensation but also may have a *skeletal* somatic marker. In addition, it also has an *autonomic* marker related to increased—or decreased—pulse, blood pressure, rate of respiration, skin circulation, and so on. These autonomic and skeletal markers are usually felt in our external body—the muscles, skin, face, fingers, toes, and so on. Becoming attuned to the varying body states that we call "feelings" can be an extremely useful tool. By scanning the *felt sense*—the status of our body related to visceral, skeletal, or autonomic sensations—we can interpret our well-being related to stresses, conflicts, and trauma in our lives. Observing our sensory body map during meditation is a powerful tool in finding and sustaining the presence that is the essence of mindfulness. Body-based psychotherapy techniques, such as Peter Levine's somatic experiencing, use the graded and balanced exploration of somatic markers to gently approach and extinguish somatic procedural memories linked to a traumatic experience.

The frontal, or anterior, insula stores visceral sensations/markers—those arising from the mouth, throat, abdominal organs, heart, and lungs. The posterior insula, on the other hand, relates to somatic sensations/markers—those related to the skeletal muscles, joints, ligaments, extremities, and autonomic control of skin circulation. The insula therefore provides a link between painful sensations and the emotions they evoke. It also has close links to the anterior cingulate gyrus and is involved in regulating the autonomic nervous system, promoting homeostasis.

Both the anterior region of the cingulate and the insula participate in establishing the meaning of events and of the somatic markers arising from them. This may provide the link between the visceral feeling and its emotional meaning, allowing us to interpret the feeling and make use of it. It's possible that this mechanism may contribute to the apparent link between these two brain centers and the process of sustaining homeostasis. Along with the anterior cingulate and OFC, the insula is activated during experiences correlating with empathy and attunement, and it appears to take part in Porges's social engagement system, discussed later. Finally, the insula seems to play a role in addictions, which I will explore in the next section. The more we learn about it, the more it seems that the insula may be unique in its capacity for providing a window into consciousness, awareness of our internal states and feelings, and therefore our basic sense of self.

An important region of the right frontal cortex overlying the skull eye socket, the *orbitofrontal cortex* (OFC) is thought to be closely connected with the process of maternal-infant bonding and affiliation with the infant, tribe, or family. Psychologist Allan Schore proposed that the right OFC is the primary link to the physical and emotional process of attunement and bonding between the mother and infant. He proposes a physical, eye-to-eye link between the mother and infant that sustains homeostasis and promotes actual growth of the OFC in the infant.

During the nursing process, one can see a direct continuous eye/facial contact between both bonding participants. Nursing often begins instinctually at the left breast, affording a right-eye to right-eye connection between mother and infant, connecting their right OFCs. As a result of this process of bonding, the OFC in the infant actually grows in size during the first months of life, overlapping the frontal tip of the left frontal cortex. This can be measured on fMRI scans and is a dramatic example of neuroplasticity.

The OFC functions as a primary regulator of the amygdala, inhibiting it and putting a lid on the autonomic nervous system if the content of a threatening experience is minor. So the OFC acts as a primary player in autonomic and emotional regulation, and therefore is, with the anterior cingulate and insula, a primary regulator of homeostasis. But in the face of real and serious threat, as informed by the amygdala, the OFC will initiate the physical action of fight/flight through the motor cortex, the hypothalamus and endocrine system, and the sympathetic autonomic nervous system (see Figure 3.1).

Functional MRI studies of the brain in infants who have been abandoned, placed in orphanages, or otherwise poorly attuned because of mental illness in the mother reveal that the size of the OFC—and of the hippocampus—is selectively smaller. This poorly developed OFC would predict that the infant is likely to face a lifetime of impairment of regulation of emotions and the autonomic nervous system, the opposite of homeostasis. And this state would most likely correlate with attachment disorders; speech, language, and learning disorders; and disturbed emotional and autonomic function in these children. This finding is a classic example of negative neuroplasticity, the physical malleability of the brain in stress, which will be the topic of Key 5.

Another fascinating, but still unproven, model for affiliation, empathy, and social connections involving part of the emotional brain is that of *mirror neurons.* Mirror neurons were first documented in the early 1990s when neuroscientists measured neuronal firing in the motor cortex of monkeys with electrodes. They found that these motor neurons fired not only when the monkey reached with a hand for food, but also when it *saw* another monkey reach with its hand for food. In other words, the brain *mirrored* a motor action when seeing the same action in another. Subsequent studies revealed clusters of mirror neurons in various areas in the motor and somatosensory cortexes, especially those representing the hand. In addition to these areas, the anterior cingulate, insula, and OFC also are rich sources of mirror neurons. This relationship of mirror neurons with the emotional brain may support the concept of the emotional connection of empathy—personally identifying with the perceived emotional state of another. Although the precise role of mirror neurons is still in debate, many feel that they specifically relate to empathy, affiliation, and bonding.

Finally, neuroscientist Stephen Porges has postulated a complex but compelling argument for what he calls a mammalian "social engagement system." This function in many ways mimics the attunement/bonding process between mother and infant related to the OFC and cingulate. This concept is built on the unique structure and function of voluntary muscle systems of the head and neck, the dorsal (reptilian) and ventral (mammalian) vagal nuclei in the brainstem, and the fight/flight/freeze response. We've danced around this concept several times now, but it's worth pulling it together as a whole. The social engagement system explains much about our daily physical/emotional behavior, and what brain centers and systems drive it.

The system begins in the motor cortex, with nerve pathways that control the eye muscles (*looking*), facial muscles (*emotional expression*), middle-ear muscles (*selecting for sounds of the human voice*), jaw muscles (*chewing*), muscles of the larynx and throat (*vocal emphasis, or prosody*), and head-turning muscles (*orienting*). These muscles, as you'll recall, are derived from the embryonic gill arches and are closely linked to survival. All of them contribute to communication, through facial expression and its meaning, speech patterns that contain inviting vocal expressions, tuning of hearing for the human voice, and orienting to the person being engaged socially.

The centers for these muscles in the brainstem are clustered around the ventral vagal nucleus, or *nucleus ambiguus*, the mammalian vagus that modulates the autonomic nervous system. They have close and intimate connections with the ventral vagus in order to contribute to its basic role in sustaining homeostasis. This role is extremely complex, but put simply, the ventral vagus inhibits the extremes of the fight/flight response, and inhibits the dangerous plunge into the dorsal vagal freeze response. You'll recall that the opposite of homeostasis is the sustained exaggerated cycling between sympathetic and parasympathetic extremes. The ventral vagus, through inhibiting these extremes, is thus another engine of homeostasis. The social engagement system, operating through the critical muscles of the head and neck that promote attunement and engagement with another person, provides the interactive communication system that physically contributes to maintenance of homeostasis.

Reward Systems and Pleasure:
The Natural "High"

Certain behaviors are important for survival in all animals, particularly mammals because of the complexity of behavior that's fostered by their more complex brains. Reptiles rely solely on the primitive instincts from their hind brain. Instincts are not amenable to learning on the go and are not capable of rapidly changing adaptive behavior based on the nature of survival challenges. As a result, the mortality rate of maturing reptiles is extremely high, necessitating huge numbers of progeny for the species to survive. For a species to survive with the smaller reproductive capacity of mammals, it must develop far more complex behavioral capacities.

Mammals have the benefit of the limbic brain, which allows a wider range and complexity of options for survival behavior. Although much of survival behavior is unconscious, as I've noted, there still are many options for the unconscious mammalian brain to choose. Most of these are based on accumulated experience, governed by conditioned experience and response, and stored in procedural memory. As you'll recall, Pavlov's dogs "learned" to salivate when a bell rang because it was associated with food, a prime survival experience that acted as a reward. Sometimes conditioned learning in Pavlov's lab was associated with a *negative* experience, such as a shock or pain that subsequently taught the dog survival behavior in the form of avoidance. But much of survival learning is based on internal reward systems that have evolved along with the emotional limbic brain. These reward systems are based on the brain's neurotransmitters, chemicals that promote message transfer from neuron to neuron. And not surprisingly, most of the neurotransmitters that provide reward are primarily within the emotional brain and its connections.

We can probably best describe the reward that is provided by these neurotransmitters as *pleasure*, an experience quite vague and difficult to describe or define, but one that we all immediately recognize. It encompasses many positive emotional states—contentment, satisfaction, enjoyment, happiness, delight, joy, and ecstasy, to name a few. And, of course, as a "feeling" along this list of increasingly intense states of pleasure, each reward-based emotional state is associated with a predictable visceral and somatic sensory experience that enhances the reward. One can see how such a system would have a powerful effect on survival behavior.

The primary brain center that is associated with an emotional state

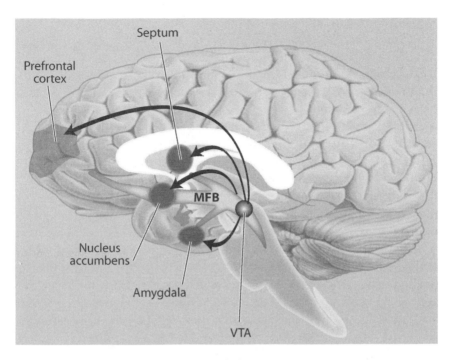

Figure 4.1 Centers of the Brain for Reward/Pleasure

of pleasure is the *nucleus accumbens* (see Figure 4.1). The nucleus accumbens is located in the region of the basal ganglia, discussed in Key 1, the centers for balance and coordination. Among other things, the accumbens plays a role in reward, pleasure, addiction, and the placebo effect. The accumbens is in close connection with the *ventral tegmental area* (VTA), a group of neurons in the mid-brain that is linked to the accumbens by the neurotransmitter *dopamine.*

Dopamine has many varied and important functions. These include motivation, mood, cognitive performance, skilled movement patterns, and reward (food, sex, drugs). Most importantly for this discussion, dopamine is released in large amounts from the VTA when a person has taken amphetamines, nicotine, or cocaine, triggering the pleasure mediated by the accumbens. So, despite its numerous essential functions, dopamine also plays a major role in addictions through these reward processes. The body is finely tuned to the presence and functions of its own chemicals. When one takes corticosteroids for such inflammatory diseases as rheumatoid arthritis or asthma, the adrenal glands balance the body by reducing their production of cortisol. In the same manner, when one takes a drug that mimics the function of a brain neurotransmitter, the neural connections using that neurotransmitter lower their production, so that when the levels of the external drug drop, the brain function of that neurotransmitter is depleted. This causes a state of "withdrawal," with numerous side effects from the suppressed and reduced neurotransmitter brain function. The response is called an "addiction," a continuing craving for that addictive substance. It's also associated with physical symptoms of withdrawal—unpleasant and painful symptoms, particularly within the viscera—when access to the substance is stopped. Therefore, dopamine is often called the "addiction" brain chemical. But dopamine is just the messenger, not the culprit. When a drug is substituted for dopamine, the normal "pleasure" of motivation, sharp thinking, and optimal mood has been replaced by the bludgeoning and overwhelming "high" of addiction.

Most other "addictive drugs"—nicotine, alcohol, cocaine, amphetamines, and opiates such as heroin—operate at least in part by stimulating the neurons in the VTA and causing release of dopamine by the ventral tegmentum to activate the accumbens. In other words, the "pleasure" experience is secondary to that of dopamine itself. Opiates produce a "rush" initially, which is related to this dopamine release, but then sustain a sense of calm relaxation. But the addictive quality of the dopamine rush remains the primary addictive feature of opiates. This quality of dopamine also seems to contribute to other addictive drugs, such as alcohol and nicotine, as their pleasure-producing quality also depends at least in part on dopamine. But sedative drugs, such as alcohol and the tranquilizers, or benzodiazepines (Valium, Xanax), also act by mimicking the inhibitory neurotransmitter gamma amino butyric acid (GABA). GABA inhibits arousal triggered by the amygdala, and withdrawal from benzodiazepines, as with alcohol, is characterized by jitteriness, hyperarousal, and even possibly seizures. Addiction therefore is based on co-opting the role of specific neurotransmitters, leaving the brain deprived of essential message symptoms, resulting in negative neuroplasticity and dysfunctional restructuring of brain pathways.

The medical field that studies and treats addictions has struggled with the basic concepts of how people become addicted to external substances, and why. We know that alcoholism tends to run in families, and there's some preliminary evidence that there may be a specific gene that predisposes one to become an alcoholic. But then we must struggle with the emerging science of epigenetics, implying that early life experience, even before birth, may be necessary to "switch on" that gene. Lately the concept of the "addictive personality" has emerged yet again, positing that certain types of personality features we're born with make us more susceptible to addiction. Many psychologists think that we're born with genetically determined *temperaments* — basically either "sensitive" or "resilient." If we're sensitive, we're prone to be vulnerable to negative life events; if resilient, we're less vulnerable. The quality of the mother's capacity to bond and attune may affect the personality features that we develop throughout our childhood, including, perhaps, the addictive personality. Whether we look at the problem from the standpoint of epigenetics, or from negative life experiences in infancy and early childhood, we end up not with the addictive *personality*, but rather with the addictive *brain*.

I would suggest that the addictive brain is simply the brain that, through late pregnancy stress, impaired early attunement, early infancy medical problems, family discord, childhood medical problems, or any other early life stress or trauma, is subject to the impaired autonomic/emotional regulation that we've been discussing. The addictive brain is constantly seeking means of calming, of shutting down the amygdala in an effort to achieve stability and peace. The so-called drugs of addiction basically all have those properties, but exact a painfully high price. Academic studies have increasingly linked early childhood negative life experiences and trauma with the later potential for addiction, as evidenced in the psychology literature and the content of addiction meetings and workshops.

Endorphins are also a well-known class of chemicals that provide pleasure and reward. They are very similar in structure to opium from the opium poppy plant. Narcotics like morphine, methadone, and codeine are derived from opium. Like opium-derived narcotics, endorphins are powerful analgesics, or pain-killing chemicals.

Endorphins are more of a hormone than a neurotransmitter in that they are released from the hypothalamus and pituitary gland into the blood stream. There they bind to endorphin receptors in the brain and spinal cord and act primarily as an analgesic. Endorphins induce a sense of pleasure in such experiences as vigorous exercise ("runner's high"), eating peppery food, a state of excitement, and sexual orgasm. They also can be induced by both the fight/flight reflex and the vagal freeze state, where they allow the animal or person to continue the act of surviving without being distracted by pain. Deep relaxation, meditation, and acupuncture are known to prompt the release of endorphins from the hypothalamus and to provide pleasure.

Endorphins probably produce pleasure by several mechanisms. They have intrinsic effects by themselves that produce calming and pleasure. Both the body's own endorphins, as well as external opioid drugs such as morphine, trigger release of dopamine from the VTA, stimulating the accumbens and causing pleasure. This dual system may account for the significant addiction risk in manufactured narcotics. And it also may account for the addictive feature of some behaviors, such as extreme athletics or risk taking, that trigger endorphin release by the hypothalamus.

The other major reward system within the brain involves the hormone *oxytocin*. As opposed to a neurotransmitter, oxytocin is a hormone secreted by the pituitary gland, and it does not cross the blood-brain barrier from the circulation. However, it clearly has significant effects on brain function, and some researchers think that there may be oxytocin synapses in the brain also. There clearly are many receptor sites in the nuclei of the limbic brain for oxytocin, including the amygdala and the accumbens.

Oxytocin has recently been referred to as the "love hormone." One of its main functions is in the birthing process. It relaxes the cervix, stimulates uterine contraction, and stimulates milk production and the "let-down" of milk by the breast. It is associated with states of pleasure around one's mate, and it promotes sexual arousal and orgasm. It facilitates calmness and maternal-infant bonding. Many believe that it enhances social engagement, as described by Porges.

Endnote

We've talked more about the mammalian, emotional brain than any other system or brain region, and for a good reason. Although the cerebral hemispheres are vastly larger than the limbic system, we spend more time in the limbic brain than in any other region, including a good part of the time we spend in sleep. The unique complex capacities of the cortex in human beings, and probably in other higher primates, have provided a huge leap in functions that involve "thinking." The capacity for intuition, insight, judgment, intention, imagination, and other higher cortical functions have created the literary, governmental, scientific, and engineering wonders of our present world.

But the limbic-based social engagement system that allows us to relate effectively and meaningfully as members of a family, tribe, or social group is probably far more important than the incredible achievements of the cortex. This system revolves around the unspoken messages served by the muscles of the head and neck, allied with the ventral vagal nucleus complex, that help with spoken and unspoken social communication. It also depends upon the OFC, the limbic nuclei, the anterior cingulate, and the insula, all of which also serve as modulators of the amygdala. Disruption of these critical limbic capacities for engagement, which are the basis of how we function in family and society, would leave us with a relatively unregulated amygdala, overreacting to innocuous cues from the environment and from the body itself. Higher cortical functions surrender to the necessity for survival, and basically shut down until the threat is past. So what we're left with is what we call mental illness, with inappropriate emotional states, and inhibition especially of the left side of the brain and its higher functions, such as speech, insight, problem solving, and judgment. The cortex therefore relies on a healthy, functional emotional brain to do its work.

PART III

HOW EXPERIENCE CHANGES OUR BRAIN, FOR BETTER OR FOR WORSE

KEY 5

THE PLASTIC, CHANGING BRAIN

I already touched briefly on the concept of neuroplasticity, the capacity for physical brain change, when I mentioned the enhanced growth of the right orbitofrontal cortex (OFC) in attuned, nurtured infants. Although until recently methods of actually looking at the brain were quite limited, many scientists speculated that the brain must be changing in some tangible way to account for selective learning of complex verbal, memory, and motor skills. The general consensus was that learning involved the strengthening of existing neural connections. This probably occurs through increased numbers of synapses between *dendrites* (nearby neuronal sprouts) and *axons* (fibers to distant neurons). I also was taught over 40 years ago in medical-school neurophysiology that the brain's allotment of neurons was fixed at birth, and only declined (without replication) throughout the life span. Now we know that the infant brain actually *parcellates*, or sheds millions of neurons in the first year of life, and also that neurons are capable of multiplying in certain brain areas throughout the life span.

In fact, there are many ways that the brain physically changes. Replication as well as death of neurons may occur through the changing chemical constitution of the body brought about by stress. New brain pathways can be formed through repetitive exposure to new information, and through practicing movement patterns and acquiring new skills, as discussed in Keys 1 and 2. The brain may be changed for the better or worse through a broad spectrum of experiences and through the influence of a relatively recently discovered genetic mechanism, the *epigenome*. And, of course, new brain pathways can grow through therapy while recovering from physical damage such as stroke or brain injury. As you can see, a lot of what we're talking about is the process of *learning*. All of what we refer to as learning, whether it's physical or cognitive, is based on principles of neuroplasticity. And as you'll also see, all of what we refer to as "trauma," and all of the things that promote healing of emotional and physical wounds, involve this exciting and expanding concept of the changing brain.

The Brain's Heritage Revisited:
Newsflash! We Can Grow New Neurons!

Early neuroscientists believed what I was taught in medical school—that the brain receives its allotment of neurons in infancy, and thereafter creates no more. But in the 1960s several investigators definitively proved that new neurons were routinely created (neurogenesis) in part of the hippocampus, and also in neuronal pathways for smell, the olfactory bulb. These studies were initially done in canaries, and then rats, using a radioactively tagged protein, thymidine, an essential part of our genetic DNA molecule. The investigators discovered many tagged neurons that must have developed since the thymidine injection, powerful evidence for neurogenesis. The new neurons appeared to be developing from neuronal stem cells, not from actual division of existing neurons.

But science learns slowly, and these findings were ignored or denied until the 1980s, when other neuroscientists discovered very clear-cut neurogenesis through division of neurons in rats, birds, and monkeys, again with the use of thymidine tagging. As these techniques became more refined in the 1990s, investigators began to study neurogenesis along with environmental variables, especially the effects of an "enriched environment," exercise, and mental challenges. Not surprisingly, prompting mice to run mazes, providing access to a running wheel, and physical handling of the mice all resulted in a marked increase in hippocampal cortex thickness, and even in the number of neuron replications. And this even occurred in older mice. Clearly mental and physical stimulation are a potent stimulus for brain growth.

The study in humans generated great interest, as one would expect. A group of Swedish researchers obtained permission from terminal cancer patients to inject radioactively tagged chemicals with compounds that had an affinity for newly generated neurons. When the patients died and were autopsied, the researchers documented tagged neurons in the hippocampus in virtually all of the patients' brains—neurons that had formed even as the patient was dying from cancer. Subsequent researchers have confirmed these findings, and many have postulated that neurogenesis probably occurs in many regions of the brain, including the neocortex, although this hasn't been documented yet. But the hippocampus makes a lot of sense as a focus for neurogenesis, given its role in conscious declarative memory consolidation of information as part of the lifelong learning process. The implications of neurogenesis as part of neuroplasticity are mind-boggling. Chemical factors that stimulate neurogenesis should have profound implications for treatment of neurodegenerative diseases such as Alzheimer's, Parkinson's, ALS, and multiple sclerosis.

Neuroscientists have also found that elevated levels of the stress hormone cortisol cause neuronal loss and atrophy, or shrinkage, specifically of the hippocampus in mice and other lab animals. Perhaps the vulnerability of the hippocampus to cortisol is a measure of how plastic its neurons really are. Functional MRI studies of the brain in abused children also show selective shrinkage of the hippocampus, and not surprisingly, deficits in attention, memory, and cognitive function have also been documented in abused children. But even mice that had been exposed to stress, with resulting hippocampal shrinkage, recovered normal size of the hippocampus with exercise and a generally enriched environment. Depression in humans is associated with memory deficits and sleep disorders, and also appears to cause atrophy of the hippocampus on fMRIs. Depression, of course, can be treated by antidepressant drugs such as Prozac in both humans and "depressed" (stressed) mice. In fact, Prozac indeed appears to reverse hippocampal atrophy in both mice and depressed humans. So here we have a means of diminishing or possibly even reversing the effects of negative neuroplasticity in stress, depression, and possibly even Alzheimer's disease through brain-stimulation activities.

Train the Brain, Enlarge the Brain: Neurons that Fire Together Wire Together

Although growth or shrinkage of parts of the brain may reflect gain or loss of neurons, there's more to it than that. It's now clear that this change in size is more a measure of the increase or decrease in the number and volume of nerve fibers, or axons, as well as an increase in the number of synapses, or connections between neurons and their fibers. You'll recall an example of this type of brain plasticity in newborn infants who are nurtured and attuned versus those raised in an orphanage. The attuned infants show measurable increased physical growth and size of the right orbitofrontal cortex (OFC) compared to their abandoned counterparts. This is a great example of a very specific life experience having a very specific effect on a specific brain region. The clinical/behavioral result of optimal attunement, then, is that of lifelong optimal emotional and autonomic homeostasis, a perfect model for plasticity.

London cab drivers—or New York cabbies, for that matter—must develop a detailed memory for the map of the city's streets. This requires significantly increased function in the memory-storing hippo-campus, especially the posterior region that stores spatial memories. Functional MRIs in the London group showed substantial increase in size and thickness of the posterior hippocampus, but actually smaller size of the anterior hippocampus, the area for *new* memory storage, which they didn't have to use as much. The cabbies also tested more poorly than average for memory for new information. After retirement, their hippocampus returned to normal size. They no longer needed the many new brain pathways that they had developed under the demand for spatial memory that their careers had required.

The process by which new connections between neurons, or rewir-ing, takes place is still theoretical. Over 50 years ago, neuroscientist Donald Hebb developed the concept that if two neurons fired at the same time, their synapses would be strengthened, and they would then begin to fire together, strengthening their synaptic connections even further. This concept evolved into the theory of *long-term potentiation*. In other words, the nerve fibers of these neurons that fired simulta-neously would increase both in number and in their capacity to fire together, a physical model for the process of learning. This process in-volves a number of complex neurotransmitters that help the ease of synapses firing within this potentiated circuit. The more consistent the triggering of this neuronal firing is, the more the physical connection grows and consolidates, a dynamic model for learning. This applies to every facet of learning—motor skills, long-term memory, and even the implicit procedural learning related to trauma. A good example of long-term potentiation is the process of classical conditioning described in Key 2.

The brain center that is probably the most sensitive to this process of shrinking and growing with experience is, not surprisingly, the hippo-campus, the center for declarative memory and events, including words, images, emotions, sensations, and so on. There are several ways to en-hance declarative-memory retention by the hippocampus. One is to get a good night's sleep. One function of sleep is to consolidate and retain short-term memory to make it long-term. Memory consolidation is one of the primary functions of rapid eye movement (REM) or dream sleep. That's why dreams often directly represent events of the day mixed up with often bizarre memories from the past. Measuring dream sleep states during a nocturnal EEG reveals increased REM activity if the day before was spent on intensive learning or study, or for that matter on intense physical or emotional activity. A good night's sleep is essential for effective memory consolidation. On the flip side, poor sleep impairs memory retention and learning. Disrupted sleep patterns are often seen in clinical depression, an emotional state characterized by impaired memory and also progressive shrinkage of the hippocampus, probably due to increased serum cortisol levels. In such a case, we could say that neurons that fire apart wire apart.

There are a number of ways to enhance the process of storing declarative memory, or learning (i.e., wiring together). One is *repetition*, the simplest and most commonly used for new learning. Functional MRIs of medical students have shown that their parietal lobe thickness increased measurably after a period of intense study that primarily involved repetition. In medical school, I found that learning was primarily a process of rote memorization of a vast volume of esoteric and often relatively unrelated words, concepts, and ideas. My classmates and I knew that only a small percentage would ever be permanently retained in memory and that such retention would depend on what medical specialty we ultimately chose. But many of these esoteric facts were part of our expanding general knowledge, and all had to be retained if we wanted to do well on the next test. So we would spend hours in exercises of rote repetition, rereading textbooks and lecture notes and grilling each other on the accumulating mountain of unrelated facts.

A second technique is to form associations of the new information with old information that has been recorded effectively in our long-term memory. This is accomplished by a process known as *elaboration*. Elaboration helps to store declarative memory by linking it with important memories already stored on a long-term basis. One way to do this is by establishing a *meaning* for the memory to be stored. For example, your ability to remember the name of Chicago's Wrigley Building would be enhanced by linking the name to the concept of your favorite chewing gum. This linking by association is a common, often unconscious means of memory elaboration. Another means is to link the memory to an emotional state or to an aspect of your past life. For example, if you're trying to remember that your new boss's birthday is on December 14th, you might link December with long-term memories of happy childhood Christmases, and the number 14 with the age you were when you had your first kiss. These emotions and aspects of our past life constitute our *autobiographical* memory, which is relatively hard-wired and therefore easily retrievable.

Finally, the use of *mnemonics* is a useful way to enhance recall through elaboration. Mnemonics are especially useful when the information to be remembered has no common meaning, is detailed, and is also fairly random. One good example is the universal mnemonic for the musical notes on the lines of the treble clef—EGBDF—the mnemonic for which is Every Good Boy Does Fine. The bass clef, GBDFA, is recalled through the mnemonic Good Boys Do Fine Always. Medical students are famous for the rampant use of mnemonics in trying to elaborate and store unrelated memory lists, particularly the names of branches of major arteries, nerves arising from nerve trunks, and otherwise unrelated names. Given our penchant for the arcane, and more often the raunchy, my classmates and I vied with each other for developing the most risqué mnemonics for these hard-to-memorize lists. I'll leave those to the reader's vivid and perhaps bawdy imagination.

The Plasticity of Brain Maps: New Pathways that Compensate for Lost Ones

The organization of the cerebral cortex has often been referred to as a *brain map*. Precise, supposedly unchangeable regions of the brain were mapped out by neuroscientists early in the 20th century, particularly by Charles Sherrington. As I was taught in medical school, these maps were believed to be relatively identical from person to person. The term *brain maps* implies that specific regions of the cortex, especially the sensory cortex, relate to specific functions that are the same in all human brains. This concept has given rise to the concept of the *homunculus*, which presents as a map of the human body overlying the motor and sensory cortices (see Figure 1.2 on page 17). Note from the figure that the size of the representation of various parts of the body varies a great deal. One of the two most important functions that have evolved in the human species is speech (hence the huge part of the cortex devoted to the mouth and tongue). The second is the ability of the thumb to cross over, or oppose, the other fingers, which provided unique new functions for hand dexterity. So the tongue and thumb representations on the motor cortex homunculus (their brain maps) are both disproportionately large.

Scientists have developed techniques to measure brain maps over the exposed cortex of monkeys with increasing precision. With time, they've discovered that with sustained practice or training involving specific parts of the body, the brain map will actually increase in size. By the same token, relative disuse will shrink the brain map representing the neglected body part. That's why prolonged immobilization in a cast, or other types of reduced use, such as that caused by pain, will reduce the size of the brain map for the impaired part of the body. It will also impair the skilled use of the neglected body part. I used to see this frequently in my rehabilitation center in patients with physical injuries to bones and joints requiring prolonged immobilization, or paralysis of limbs from temporary impairment of peripheral nerves not related to brain injury. These patients had lost motor skills — it was as if their brain had "forgotten" not only the skill but also the arm or leg itself! Fortunately, brain plasticity also allowed the patients to regain strength and skills through fairly detailed retraining and recovery of the "forgotten limb" and its brain map representation. Although I didn't realize it then, restoring functional brain maps was the primary accomplishment of many rehabilitation procedures, even for impairment not related to neurological deficits or injuries.

Researcher Michael Merzenich (see Sharon Begley in the Recommended Reading section) is a pioneer in the study of neuroplasticity. Using minuscule electrodes on the exposed brain, he developed a method of measuring and charting brain maps in monkeys with exquisite accuracy and detail. Redrawing the brain map takes place through a number of different mechanisms. One remarkable way that the brain responds to brain injury is by the area of the cortex adjacent to the damage beginning to take over the lost function. Merzenich caused a stroke that destroyed the area of the cortex that represented the hand in monkeys. As the monkeys recovered, the brain map next to the damage began to expand and incorporate the map for the paralyzed hand. As the monkey began to use the paralyzed hand more, the brain map continued to increase in size, even though it originally didn't represent the hand.

Blocking message transfer through peripheral nerves also will cause a change in the corresponding brain map. Merzenich cut the median nerve in monkeys, and later discovered that both the motor and sensory brain maps representing that nerve disappeared. When he measured the brain map for the rest of the hand, which was served by the remaining ulnar and radial nerve of the hand, he found that the maps for these two nerves had expanded to include the missing median nerve motor and sensory maps. When he removed a finger from a monkey, the brain maps for the adjacent two fingers expanded to incorporate the map for the lost finger.

The same phenomenon can also take place in reverse. When a person with "webbed" fingers, a congenital abnormality, has them surgically separated, what was once a single common brain map for both fingers separates into two individual brain maps. In other studies, cutting the sensory pathways in the spinal cord serving the hand in monkeys caused the facial brain map (the face lies next to the hand on the homunculus) to expand and take over the hand area. So in all of these studies, both damage to the brain and cutting off the sensory message system of a body part results in adjacent brain regions taking over some of the function of the body part that lost its brain representation. This remarkable plasticity probably explains the significant degree of recovery that one often sees in patients who have recovered function following stroke, brain injury, or injury to peripheral nerve pathways.

Sometimes brain maps take over entirely different functions. The visual, or occipital, cortex in the back of the brain is activated when someone reads a book. Functional MRIs in blind individuals who learn to read Braille show that the occipital cortex is activated by the Braille reading, even though the sensory signal is related to touch and proprioception (position sense), not vision. The brain map has been moved to a totally different region, and the sensory signal activating it has totally changed. All of these studies suggest that the brain is far more plastic than we thought and that the concept of a fixed brain representation for specific body parts (the homunculus) is vastly oversimplified.

Epigenetics:
Turning Genes On and Off

Our genes affect who and what we are in many ways, some glaringly obvious, others hidden and mysterious. Hair, eye, and skin color, straight or curly hair, height, body structure—these genetic gifts are grossly obvious and taken for granted. Intelligence, musical ability, and certain other talents are less obvious but also basically genetically determined. Many genes are also either dominant or recessive—more or less likely to be expressed, and reflecting which parent has the dominant gene for which trait.

Genes also reflect traits that affect our health and well-being. Many diseases are carried in genes that generally are more subtle and subject to lifestyle and environmental factors. These include diabetes, heart disease, hypertension, and cancer, among many others. Expression of these genes significantly depends upon lifestyle choices, and may be mitigated by patterns of behavior that minimize the expression of the gene. Eating a diet low in fats, calories, and salt may mitigate the expression of a genetic tendency for obesity, diabetes, coronary artery disease, or hypertension. Many psychiatric disorders also appear to have a genetic tendency, including schizophrenia, bipolar disorder, alcoholism, and the autism spectrum. Alzheimer's disease is linked to a genetic trait, but factors that set off that trait are still uncertain. Finally, there are a number of diseases, most of them neurological, that are purely genetic, where possession of the gene by one or both parents guarantees the development of the disease. A few examples are cystic fibrosis, types of muscular dystrophy, Huntington's disease, and Tay-Sachs disease.

In recent years, however, studies in genetic inheritance have begun to show that certain types of life experience seem to affect members of families several generations down the line in mysterious and unexpected ways. These findings have cast considerable doubt on our assumptions about the inevitability of our genetic heritage. They suggest that other, previously unidentified factors are at work here.

Back in the 1980s, a Swedish preventive health specialist, Dr. Lars Bygren, became interested in a period during the 19th century that was characterized by an extremely variable access to food, with periods of famine interspersed with times of relative plenty. Bygren had the insight to study what implications these events might have on subsequent generations. His findings were startling. They showed that both extremes of diet—gluttony and malnourishment—in grandparents could result in heart disease, diabetes, and shortened life spans in the grandchildren. This unusual passage of traits even extended to the period of time the fetus spent in the womb. Mothers with poor diets during the period of gestation produced children who were more prone to heart disease as adults. Somehow, these two extremes of diet during a critical period in life changed the genetic heritage enough to affect health in several generations down the line. This was a powerful blow to the universally accepted concept of Darwinian generational evolution through means that ensured the survival of the fittest.

Subsequent studies have confirmed these unusual transgenerational findings. Smoking and obesity in parents has now been shown to pass on obesity and shorter life span to the children. Studies of separated identical twins have shown remarkable similarities between the twins despite their having been raised in different households, but we've also known for some time that even with the same genes, identical twins may differ significantly with regard to diseases and physical and mental health. In the field of trauma, an increased incidence of PTSD, depression, and suicide has been documented in children and grandchildren of Holocaust survivors. Researchers have speculated that this finding could be the result of an impaired capacity in traumatized parents for nurturing and bonding. But now the possibility of genetic transcription as a causative factor must be considered in posttraumatic generational trauma as well. For generations, scientists have operated on the assumption that DNA, the genetic material that governs our genetic inheritance, is stable, unchangeable, and inevitable, and that it determines the transmission of traits. Darwin has been assumed to be right. But these findings have seriously challenged this basic assumption.

In the past decade or so it has become apparent that external forces can "switch on" or "switch off" parts of our DNA genetic code, a process called *transcription*. And once changed, that altered code can continue to be passed on for generations. These findings support and explain Bygren's earlier findings. The term *epigenome* has been given to this changeable structure, but the epigenome actually is a chemical change, not a tangible entity. The area of potential chemical change on the genetic structure that we consider to be the epigenome has been called a "mark," and it appears to be able to turn the gene on or off to make a protein. One of the primary processes in this change involves *DNA methylation*, or addition of a chemical *methyl group* to the gene, implying a change in its basic chemistry. Such a changed gene is called im*printed*. Imprinting such a gene defies the usual expectation of a gene being dominant or recessive, and rather may make one parent—mother or father—the important factor in the gene's expression. And the change in that gene may be passed down to one gender for several generations. It's of interest that maternal genes tend to suppress growth, and paternal to enhance it, which has implications for passage of tendencies for cancer and other illnesses characterized by rapid growth.

It's clear that the role of genetic inevitability, gene dominance, and gender all need to be rethought, but scientists don't believe that epigenetics will replace the concept of Darwinian natural selection. These new findings basically add an additional and very important level of complexity to the process of inheritance. The finding that experience can affect one's genes, not only for one but also for perhaps many generations, has profound implications, especially in the fields of behavioral science, medicine, and neuroplasticity. For decades, medical science has focused on the traditional DNA-based genetic tendencies for the specific diseases I've discussed. But attempts to change genomes by external means in order to prevent or cure disease have so far been unsuccessful. Nevertheless, much more adaptable and changeable methods of epigenetic manipulation may hold promise for the future.

Healing the Injured Brain: Using Neuroplasticity to Recover Lost Function

It's fortunate that the brain is far more resilient than we've been taught to believe, because it's also a rather vulnerable organ system—it's basically about three pounds of soft, gelatinous tissue stored in a fairly sturdy rigid container. Yet it has incredible complexity of form and function.

The arterial system that provides oxygen and nutrients reflects the complexity of the brain itself. Although armed with some very strategic redundant arterial pathways to provide flexibility, the system is also prone in later life to malfunction, resulting in what we call a stroke.

There are several types of circulatory impairment that can cause a stroke, and the majority of them seem to take place in an arterial system that is less resilient to obstruction than the rest, generally involving the cerebral cortex. Loss of blood supply results in the death of brain tissue in the region supplied by those arteries. The most vulnerable arterial system specifically provides blood primarily to the upper extremities, and to a lesser extent the legs. As a former rehabilitation physician, I am well aware of the challenge of rehabilitating the paralyzed arm.

Standard rehabilitation practices reflect the fact that functional recovery of the severely paralyzed arm is extremely difficult, and the functional outcomes poor to fair. Most of the therapy emphasizes learning adaptive techniques to compensate for the paralysis by special training in use of the functional arm, and exercises for balance, coordination, and mobility for the partially paralyzed leg. Treatment of the affected arm mostly involves reducing spasticity, or the stiffness that accompanies the arm paralysis and that by itself is a real impediment for use.

In the early 1980s, neuropsychologist Edward Taub studied the recovery of function in monkeys whose upper limb had been *deafferented*—deprived of all sensation by cutting only the sensory nerve to that extremity. Surprisingly, the monkey stopped using the numb arm even though the motor pathways for movement were still intact. Taub recalled an old study from the early 1900s that suggested that restraining the good arm in deafferented monkeys resulted in the monkeys beginning to use the numb arm remarkably effectively. Unfortunately his experiment was interrupted at that point by accusations from an animal rights group that he was abusing the monkeys, leading to legal proceedings that put his investigative career on hold.

Taub was eventually vindicated, and he switched his studies to human stroke patients, where he found the opportunity to study what he called "constraint-induced movement therapy." He had his stroke patients wear a restraining sling on their good arm, which prevented the good arm from taking over for the paralyzed one, and then had them do varied, rigorous, and repetitive exercises with the paralyzed arm and hand for 6 hours a day over a 2-week period. All four of Taub's patients, some of them several years post-stroke, experienced universal and relatively dramatic improvement in function of the previously paralyzed arm. Despite relative rejection by the scientific community, by 2006

Taub ultimately was able to demonstrate consistent improvement in most—but not all—of his patients. Through transcranial magnetic stimulation, Taub was able to document a sizeable increase in the brain map both around the area of the original stroke and in adjacent but more distant motor and premotor brain regions. Taub's findings are important because they show not just that brain maps enlarge with therapy and use of a body part, but also that external influences on the brain may elicit plasticity and healing—and that the window of opportunity is much longer than we realized.

Chronic pain is one of the most common and perplexing symptoms seen in physicians' offices. Some estimates suggest that over half of all visits to physicians are motivated by seeking of pain relief. Because of the nature of our training, we physicians have been taught that pain is a warning symptom of some type of pathological process that is stimulating pain receptors in some part of the body. Of course pain receptors are present in all organs of the body—skin, joints, tendons, ligaments, muscles, viscera, arteries, and so on—except in the brain tissue itself. Perception of pain is the ultimate message of danger to the well-being or life of the person or creature, and it is critical for survival. The rare syndrome of congenital insensitivity to pain is usually rapidly fatal in childhood because of the absence of awareness to pain caused by potentially fatal illnesses, such as appendicitis.

But the structural concept of the origin of pain does not explain a number of strange types of pain syndromes. Two of the most vexing and perplexing of these syndromes were actually described by an early American neurologist, Silas Weir Mitchell, working with soldiers in the Civil War. Mitchell chose names for them that are as esoteric and indecipherable as most terms for diseases: (1) phantom limb pain, and (2) reflex sympathetic dystrophy (RSD), or its newer name, complex regional pain syndrome, type I. Both of them defy medical logic in their expression of pain, may have no or minimal physical findings, and have generally been resistant to attempts at pain management. How could one feel pain in a body part that no longer existed? Yet both are relatively common, and reasonably similar from case to case.

The perception of persistence of sensation in an amputated limb is a common phenomenon. If the amputation was not associated with pain before the removal of the limb, phantom limb pain is less common. Phantom sensation—tingling, cramping—is more common, with the limb often feeling as if it is still holding the posture before the amputation. The brain map for that absent limb often spreads to other maps close by, such as the hand and the face. So an individual with an amputated hand may feel the hand when he shaves, because the homunculus mapping of the hand and the face are very close. Women who have had a premenopausal hysterectomy may still feel uterine cramps on a monthly basis. Patients whose bladders were removed for cancer may still feel painful cramping of the absent bladder, and so on. Similarly, if the person experienced severe pain in an extremity before the amputation, the phantom limb can become the source of unremitting pain, often mimicking the pre-amputation pain itself. Therapeutic interventions for phantom limb pain, including nerve blocks, or implanting electrodes in the spinal cord to block pain, have been generally unsuccessful.

Because of the intense burning quality to the pain, reflex sympathetic dystrophy (RSD) was initially called *causalgia*, based on the Greek word *causus*, meaning "to burn." RSD is a strange but consistent syndrome, as I've noted, associated with severe, burning pain usually in an extremity that has been injured. The injury may be as severe as a fracture or laceration or as benign as a minor bruise. It also is occasionally seen in the paralyzed limb after a stroke. A series of changes occurs, first with redness, warmth, and unusual hair and nail growth, followed by loss of the hair, atrophy and ridging of the nails, osteoporosis (thinning of the bones), pallor, and coldness, with contracture and deformity of the extremity. These symptoms indicate the wasting, or dystrophic, elements of the disease. Exquisite sensitivity to any touch or sensation in the involved extremity is common. Even a slight breeze on the limb may be excruciating. Early parasympathetic signs are common (redness, nail or hair growth), followed by sympathetic changes reflecting constriction of skin blood vessels that reflect the name. Many invasive surgical procedures, medications, and therapies have been tried, with variable and usually unsuccessful results.

Neuroscientist V. A. Ramachandran has studied both of these syndromes extensively. Both phantom limb pain and RSD have been shown to be associated with altered brain maps for the area representing the part of the body that is involved in the pain syndrome. Using magnetoencephalography in patients with phantom limb pain, Ramachandran demonstrated that the brain map for the upper extremity had invaded adjacent areas, especially the face, suggesting that the pain was a brain-based symptom. Similar findings were noted in patients with RSD. This certainly isn't surprising based on what we've already explored regarding brain maps and neuroplasticity. The question is whether the map is changed by the physical absence of the body part in phantom limb, or by the traumatic experience of the injury or the pain itself in RSD. The symptoms of phantom limb pain, of course, beg for a brain-based origin to the pain, especially involving those parts of the brain processing procedural memory.

In light of these findings, Ramachandran hypothesized that both RSD and phantom limb pain were based on alterations in perception of the affected or absent limb. After all, the perception of pain in an absent body part must be processed in the brain, not in the limb. He reasoned that changing the patient's perception of the affected limb might change the pain. So he devised an exquisitely simple but intuitive tool involving a box with a vertical mirror in the middle, and he had his patients place their *normal* limb in the box. When the patient saw the mirror image of the normal limb, it *looked* like the absent or painful limb but was, in fact, pain-free. And when the patient moved or manipulated the limb, it looked as if the painful or absent limb was moving. The visual image did not conform to reality, but the visual brain "perceived" the painful or absent limb to look, feel, and move normally. With repeated exposure over varying periods of time, many patients with RSD experienced disappearance of the pain and autonomic signs. In phantom limb pain, the perception of the absent limb and the pain that had accompanied it also disappeared.

Ramachandran applied the mirror-box concept to the rehabilitation of paralyzed upper extremities in stroke patients as well. Controlled scientific studies have now solidly supported the effectiveness of the mirror box in these conditions. They have established the amazing capacity of the brain for adaptation and change through plasticity.

But how could such tangible, debilitating conditions literally disappear by "fooling" the brain into changing its perception? How could such a technique "extinguish" not only subjective pain but also the objective effects of abnormal autonomic control in an extremity with RSD? What common ingredient in such diverse conditions as stroke-related paralysis, RSD with its objective signs of altered circulation, and phantom limb pain could allow these conditions to be cured without drugs or even touching the body?

I will discuss this phenomenon in more depth when I talk about trauma in Key 7, but I want to mention a few central ideas here. The way we perceive our somatic body has been shaped by many experiences in our lives. As you'll recall, somatic and visceral sensations inform the conscious brain about the integrity of the body—about safety, danger, well-being, and illness. This continuous internal feedback loop, at its best, keeps our body/mind in homeostasis. Somatic or visceral messages that convey danger *that is unresolved* will imprint these abnormal autonomic and somatic states in our survival-based procedural memory. There they are stored as a persistent and often recurring state of threat. In other words, if a particular part of the body is involved in a traumatic event and experiences pain, that sensory experience and the autonomic changes that accompany it are also stored in our survival-based procedural memory. That's classical conditioning. And memory cues of the event that triggered this whole process (usually a physical injury) will bring it back into consciousness, leading to the phantom experiences. This causes a reexperiencing of the pain, even of the absent limb, and the actual autonomic disruption (RSD) of the injured body part.

Both of these syndromes require the linking of a state of perception with unresolved danger (i.e., they are a conditioned response). So the logical treatment is *extinction*, à la Pavlov's dogs. Exposing the dogs to the bell without feeding will extinguish salivation. Repeatedly presenting the painful or absent limb as being visually normal in the mirror box will extinguish the conditioned association between the somatic pain sensations, the abnormal autonomic state, and the perception of survival in procedural memory.

Endnote

The discovery that the brain is not the static, rigid, predetermined conductor of the body's orchestra is changing not only the concept of infinite adaptability but also the concept of wellness and disease itself. The brain can shrink and grow, and new neurons can be formed, probably in areas we haven't even considered. Parts of the brain serving a specific sensory function, like vision, can adapt and serve another, like touch. Regions, or maps, of the brain that serve a specific part or region of the body can grow and incorporate other body parts or regions. And they can shrink in the face of chronic pain or physical disuse. Through mental and physical training, new pathways and neuronal connections can be formed throughout the life span. Our genetic heritage is not fixed and immutable, but rather is subject to significant change through our life experiences. By "training" the brain, objectively and functionally, through something as simple as applied classical conditioning, we can change the physical body as well.

You *can* teach an old dog new tricks. We can harness the brain's manifest plasticity and resiliency. Through environmental enrichment, physical exercise, the learning of new information, the acquiring of new skills, the treatment of depression, and the use of classical conditioning techniques, we can mitigate the effects of aging, enhance the quality of life, extinguish many types of chronic pain, and restore homeostasis.

KEY 6

THE BRAIN IN STRESS
AND TRAUMA

From this point on, I will try to bring together all that I've presented about the brain and how it works, and look more closely at how negative life experiences (stress and trauma) can alter brain function. We already opened that door a crack when we looked at how stress, through the release of *cortisol* into the blood stream, can have negative effects on both the brain and the body. Of course, when you try to wrap your mind around something really new, with unusual concepts and a strange language, your mind may have a tendency to glaze over under the assault of too much information. So a little repetition and review of some of these complex ideas seems worthwhile.

I spent some time in Key 5 exploring the boundaries of what's called *neuroplasticity*. I primarily emphasized the positive effects: the growth of brain maps, the birth of new neurons, the increase in cortical tissue through stimulation and growth of pathways, and the substitution of function by one brain area for another. But plasticity unfortunately also provides a negative mirror for all those positive potentials for growth. Plasticity most certainly can have a downside. Neurons may shrink and die; pathways may disconnect and cause impaired function. Abnormal and dysfunctional pathways may develop and grow, interfering with cognitive, emotional, and sensory-motor function. Areas of the brain that perform a specific sensory-motor function may lose track of the body part and the skill and control that they used to provide. And I'm not talking about something as severe as a stroke or tangible physical brain damage here—I'm talking about the intrinsic effects of stress and trauma on brain function.

Some of these negative changes associated with stress and trauma can be seen through imaging the brain with an MRI or CAT scan, but generally these are reliable only under significant stress in the moment. One can get an idea that something is afoot through an fMRI, which measures regional patterns of blood flow, or a PET scan, which shows regional dominance of energy utilization. These types of scans basically tell us what's "online" at any given moment—what part of the brain is burning the most glucose or has attracted the most arterial blood flow. We have a pretty good idea what function areas of the brain on either side serve. So we can guess from these scans what brain region is being used, and what function is taking place at the time of the scan. A good example, which we will return to from time to time, is what happens when danger is perceived by the sensory receptors in the head (see Key 1). We know that the amygdala is the center in the right emotional brain for warning us about danger. We also know that the other regulating nuclei (hippocampus, cingulate, OFC, and insula) will also come "on line" immediately when arousal occurs and triggers its own modulation. You'll recall that this arousal process primarily takes place in the right limbic brain. So we can expect to see the whole right limbic, emotional brain "light up" on the fMRI due to the associated shunting of blood to that area.

Conversely, we don't need words or intellectual problem solving at the first sign of danger—we need to either fight or flee. So we would expect to see a significant reduction in blood flow to the left *speech* area in the lower posterior part of the left frontal lobe, and in the "thinking" area in the left dorsal frontal cortex—which is, in fact, exactly what we see. But these are shifting, unpredictable changes based on the intensity of the experience in the moment. Admittedly, chronic stress and trauma are also associated with chronic changes in regional utilization of blood and glucose by the brain, but these are relatively unpredictable, complex, and shifting. Nevertheless, neuroscientists continue to refine their imaging techniques of the brain in stress, trauma, and mental illness.

Stress versus Trauma:
Two States, Two Responses

Stress perhaps could be defined as any physiological event, external or internal, that demands that the body adapt to it. There's a basic tension in our everyday life based on the continued need to achieve certain goals in order to survive. The most elemental needs include food, drink, shelter, and procreation. Thereafter, our basic "needs" become shaped by our cultural expectations, which are directly related to and shaped by the complexity of our culture itself. When we were hunter-gatherers on the African plains, this was pretty basic and simple. As we've moved to more complex models of cultural organization, our "basic needs" have reflected that complexity, and the definition of "stress" has proportionately broadened. Every cultural and technological advance brings new, unique stressors and demands new kinds of problem solving and adaptation. Moving from simplicity to complexity in any state of life will do that. It has taken less than a century for long-distance communication to evolve from the operator-assisted phone call to smartphones and instant international communication. Every "labor-saving" device comes at the price of effortful new learning and, if you wish, "stress." Progress is achieved through this adaptive process.

The great scientist Hans Selye (see the Recommended Reading) spent his career studying and defining stress and the nature of the body's adaptation, which he called the "general adaptation syndrome" (GAS). Many sources of stress include negative events or experiences, and survival even under the best of circumstances is associated with challenges that demand response and perhaps resolution. I suppose one could say that when circumstances present barriers to that resolution, we are experiencing true stress. Selye actually believed that some stress has a positive effect, a variant that he called "eustress," or "good" stress. But basically we can define stress by the body's reaction to it, as well as by the negative, and positive, effects of this reaction.

Striving to achieve something, defending against criticism, seeking prey as a predator, and making oneself scarce as prey could all be considered forms of stress—the important point being that all evoke a response by the brain and body that prompts the GAS. This adaptive response sets off responses from the sympathetic nervous system and the hypothalamic-pituitary-adrenal (HPA) axis that call on both the brain and the body to make specific changes to respond to and manage the stress. I discussed these effects in detail in Key 3 when I talked about the fight/flight response, understanding that stress by itself comes up short compared to full-blown fight/flight behavior. Nevertheless, stress does activate the HPA axis, the end result being exposure to elevated levels of the serum *cortisol*, which has very specific effects on the brain and the body if that exposure is prolonged. As you'll recall, cortisol causes shrinkage, or atrophy, of the brain's hippocampus. It can also cause sleep disturbance and sometimes sustained baseline arousal. From then on, the brain's response is determined by the intensity and severity of the stress and its escalating nature. The effects of stress on the body will be reviewed again in Key 7.

Trauma can be defined in a number of ways, but one way is as severe stress to the point where it becomes a threat to life. At some point in the escalation of the intensity of a stressor, the warning messages from the environment may become intense enough to activate the limbic warning center, the *amygdala*, which may turn on the fight/flight response. At this point, the sympathetic nervous system comes into play, with all of the effects of *norepinephrine* (brain neurotransmitter) on the brain and *adrenaline*, or *epinephrine* (hormone), on the body. And the brain becomes totally focused on the fight/flight response. The outcome of this experience determines whether the animal or human survives or not. Survival may be associated with escape, through flight, or successful self-defense through fighting. In some cases, when the animal or human is helpless and escape is impossible, the freeze response is reflexively produced, which may deter further attack and allow survival. In these cases, the experience of trauma depends on how the brain negotiates the freeze response itself.

The Freeze Discharge

We generally think of prey animals as being those that don't feed on other animals—rabbits, mice, and so on. But all predators also have the capacity to become prey. The ferret is the predator when he pursues the mouse, but becomes the prey when pursued by the hawk. A few "universal predators," such as sharks, lions, and polar bears, only rarely achieve prey status, such as through encounters with armed human beings, the ultimate predator.

If fighting or fleeing is useless, prey animals have one more option to fall back on: the freeze response. I discussed the freeze response extensively in Key 3, describing it as centered in the brainstem/reptilian brain. The main function of the freeze is to enable the reptile to go through a prolonged period of time with minimal expenditure of energy, minimal respiration, and profoundly slow heart rate. The purpose of this reptilian period of suspended animation is to hibernate, to dive under water to escape a predator, or to pursue prey without needing to breathe for an extended time. Without an emotional affiliative brain, reptiles aren't very selective in this area of behavior, and if the opportunity presents itself, they will eat their own kind, or their young. In the mammal, however, the freeze occurs only when the fight/flight response is no longer possible. The animal collapses in a state of immobility, with the reptilian suppression of heart rate and respiration governed by the dorsal vagal nucleus. Although useful for survival, the freeze in mammals also is dangerous because mammals rely on high energy expenditure to enhance their strong points in the game of survival—their capacity for speed and mobility. The slowing of the heart rate and respiration during the freeze, therefore, poses the possibility of death in cardiac arrest—the "voodoo death" described in Key 3.

In the human species, the freeze response can assume many faces. It's far more complex than just collapse and immobility on the ground, like the opossum, the popular model for the freeze. For instance, when shamed in public by the comments of a teacher, boss, or other dominant figure, the human will *blush*, a reddening of the face and upper body due to the dilatation of arteries that accompanies the parasympathetic freeze. Those of you who have experienced shame may recall that, for an instant, one's *mind* also freezes in the moment. The state of profound grief is also often associated with a physical collapse, numbing, and clouding of consciousness, another example of the freeze triggered by a purely emotional trauma. So the freeze may involve elements of somatosensory, visceral, and circulatory changes going on in the body. Clearly the freeze can also be triggered by "vehement emotions," where the life threat may be real but is associated with a threatening personal loss rather than with an immediate physical threat to life.

All of these complex changes provide a message for the parts of the brain that store memories, primarily the amygdala and the hippocampus, for implicit and explicit memories of the traumatic event. As you'll recall, the sensory memories from the somatic body and the organs of the chest and abdominal cavities are stored, prompted by the nature of the life threat (shame and grief both represent a threat to life or well-being). Our brain learns survival skills through this process. If the animal, opossum or human being, survives the freeze response, these survival memories need to be stored as an event *in the past*, available for future use but no longer representing imminent threat. This process of sorting out, saving, and discarding memories is achieved by a very important physiological process called the *freeze discharge*.

Many of you have probably seen a bird fly into a large, reflective window and then fall to the ground, apparently stunned. After a brief period of immobility, the bird will stagger to its feet, shake all over, and then fly away, none the worse for wear. If you were to watch the bird in slow motion, you would see that it is actually *flying in place* during the shaking, replicating the last motor action that occurred before it collapsed on the ground.

There are many video examples of this phenomenon in animals, usually from nature programs on cable television. I have a video of a polar bear shot with a tranquilizer dart from a helicopter for the purposes of tagging to collect migration information. As the bear came out of its stupor (superimposed on a freeze response), it shook all over in a manner that, when viewed in slow motion, replicated the movement of running, followed by deep sighing respirations. Footage of gazelles, frozen after being run to the ground by a cheetah, also shows replication of the motor action that preceded the freeze. This unusual and dramatic behavior, common to birds and mammals, is quite specific and stereotyped. As I mentioned, it almost always reflects the particular motor actions that the animal used as a means of attempted escape or of an attempted but failed fight response. Such relatively universal patterns of behavior must be assumed to have a purpose of some sort, especially if they are replicated throughout the species.

Psychologist Peter Levine has studied the freeze response as an animal-based instinctual process that clearly has implications for survival. In interviewing gamekeepers in Africa, he documented the critical importance of the "shaking" phenomenon in wild animals. These gamekeepers routinely tranquilize wild species for tagging and monitoring disease states and migration patterns. They commented to Levine that "if the animal does not go through the shaking, it will surely die." In these wild species, the act of the freeze response must be followed by what has been called the "discharge." Without the discharge, the animal somehow loses its survival resiliency. Some have described the shaking as the "discharge of energy."

A Corruption of Memory:
Perceiving the Past as Being the Present

There are a number of situations in which the tendency to go through the "discharge" seems to be thwarted—the animal simply does not seem to have the capacity to access this instinctual behavior. A cardinal example is zoo animals, which are subject to many diseases unique to that environment, and which often have to endure medical and surgical procedures but seldom exhibit the behavior of the discharge after those procedures. Zoo animals also tend to have a relatively shortened life span.

Laboratory animals, especially those subjected to experimental surgical procedures, seem to have the same inhibition of this natural behavior. Pavlov commented that when he took his dogs out of their cages and carried them upside down by their legs to the operating table, they remained "frozen" in the last posture they had assumed before they were laid down, with their legs fully extended just as they had been carried. He called this "animal hypnosis," although I'm sure it's clear to the reader that they were in fact in a freeze. But discharges as I've described apparently were not noted in Pavlov's dogs.

Finally, it's rare to observe this type of involuntary motor behavior in humans who live in the complex urban or suburban societies that represent the Western world. I've heard scattered anecdotes from my patients about shaking all over after an auto accident. But when this type of shaking *does* occur after an accident, passersby and even emergency technicians will try to get the person to "calm down." Obstetrical nurses have related to me frequent episodes of shaking by the mother after she has given birth. They have seen this often enough to accept it as being normal. As a culture, however, we seem to be embarrassed by unseemly, exaggerated behavior. The freeze discharge is one kind of this behavior, as is violent, vehement, or "hysterical" expression of emotions like grief or terror. Many non-Western cultures routinely support vehement expressions of grief, including ritual wailing, tearing of clothes, and falling prostrate to the ground. I would suggest that these acts of physical expression are culturally sanctioned rituals that provide a means of "discharging" the physiological element of grief and do indeed constitute the freeze response.

Recall the African gamekeepers' observations of their tagged animals' responses. They intuitively understood that the freeze discharge is life-affirming and somehow necessary for survival in the tooth-and-claw culture of the wild. If they are correct, what is the function and physiological purpose of the freeze discharge? The first clue is that the motor act of the discharge resembles the nature of the fight/flight motor activity before the freeze ensued. The amygdala ensures that all of the elements of the sensorimotor experience will be stored in procedural memory, as the episode was associated with threat. The absence of a freeze discharge, however, ensures that this memory will be stored *as if the threat is still going on.* In other words, the purpose of the freeze discharge is to *complete* the act of escape in procedural memory so that the sensorimotor activity is remembered as a survival tool *from the past—* not something that remains imminent and unresolved. By extinguishing the connection between these body memories of the attack, the failed attempts by the body to escape, and the arousal by the amygdala, the event is perceived as being over and is relegated to the past by the brain as a survival learning experience, not a persistent threat.

If the freeze discharge *doesn't* occur, all of those memories are stored as if the threat still exists, because the sensorimotor body messages of the act of flight are never extinguished. And thereafter, any cues linked in any way to the experience of the unresolved threat will trigger the arousal/fight/flight response that was never completed—at least not in procedural memory. This corruption of the perception of time—experiencing the past as being in the present—literally guarantees that the traumatic experience is destined to recur again and again, because this false procedural memory is stored in our survival bank of memories for future use. This state of persistent storage of such traumatic procedural memories as still being present, or imminent, is the substrate for what we call trauma, or PTSD.

Fear Conditioning and Kindling: Sensitizing the Brain through Conditioned Traumatic Cues

As you may have noticed, I've been emphasizing the concept of procedural memory throughout this book. That's because trauma is both a corruption of time and of memory. The procedural memories of trauma are really anything that the sensory systems of our body detected during the event. They might include:

- Smells (of bent steel and burnt rubber, or of the assailant)
- Visual images (the color of the car that hit you, the face of the assailant)
- Dizziness from the movement of your head that activated your vestibular system
- Noises (of the impact, the voice of the assailant)
- Taste (of blood)
- Sensations of pain
- Proprioception, or sense of movement of your body parts
- Reflex patterns of your body's muscle contractions for self-protection
- "Feelings," or visceral sensations, of rage, terror, despair, or grief in the belly, the pit of the stomach, the chest, or the throat

Under threat, the brain is especially finely attuned to these "somatic markers" and will store them all in procedural memory. After all, the brain might need these markers in the future to warn against threat.

And in the absence of the freeze discharge, they will be stored in our survival memory banks as being ready to recur with the faintest *cue* reminiscent of the experience. This means that *even though the event is over and we survived it,* the entire external and internal world remains a reservoir of somatic cues for what is perceived as an imminent traumatic event. In this way, trauma indeed is a corruption of the perception of time.

Exercise

This exercise may be a little risky for those of you who have had a great deal of life trauma. But the muscles that are instinctively used to protect us in states of physical threat are so universal that almost anyone could have some response to this exercise. Once again, find a comfortable chair, sit down with your hands in your lap, get comfortable, and close your eyes. Find in your past history an event that was physically threatening, such as a fall, a physical assault, or a motor vehicle accident. If you can't find one, try to remember an event when you felt physically threatened, such as physical punishment by a parent. Focus on the retained images of the event, and try to feel what happened to your body at the time it occurred. Carefully notice any tightening of muscles that accompanies this exercise. Pay particular attention to the muscles at each side of the base of your skull and neck, your jaws, and your low back. These muscles all participate in any physical act of self-defense and are likely to retain procedural memory for such events and to tighten reflexively in the face of future threats. We often tend to call them our "stress muscles." If you feel tightening of a muscle group, focus on its quality and intensity. You may actually experience twitching or movement of the muscle group, an actual freeze discharge. However, if you notice the emergence of strong emotions, take several deep breaths to regulate and modulate the process to prevent an unpleasant emotional response.

When Pavlov rang a bell and immediately fed his dogs, it took several presentations before the dogs salivated and experienced increased stomach secretions at the ringing of the bell. Classical conditioning is all about learning survival skills, and eating is one of them. One never forgets these skills completely. Even after these "skills" were extinguished by ringing the bell without feeding, years later the conditioned food-bell relationship was reestablished with just one or two presentations. Pavlov also used electric shock to condition his dogs. Pain is especially effective as a conditioning stimulus because it involves activation of the amygdala. Imprinting of procedural memories through pain or fear has been called *fear conditioning*, and it is extremely resistant to extinction. Fear conditioning is the basic mechanism in trauma, and it explains virtually all of its symptoms.

Fear conditioning not only is difficult to extinguish but also has the tendency to spread, incorporating new cues similar to the existing conditioned ones. The soldier returning from Iraq may drop to the ground with any loud noise for years even though each time the threatening noise proves to be benign. The victim of rape may panic for years upon seeing a face with any features of the rapist, such as a beard. Both the traumatized soldier and the rape victim will position themselves with their back against a wall when entering a room. They are responding to the constant tendency for cues related to the unresolved trauma to emerge, even cues that may only remotely resemble the original traumatic cues. Pavlov called this process of spread of conditioning cues *irradiation*. Victims of assault by a heavy smoker may begin to panic with any smell of smoke in their ambient environment. Victims who tried unsuccessfully to flee a threat may begin to experience panic attacks when they attempt to exercise aerobically—the increase in heart rate represents a cue to the terror of the failed attempt at flight. In other words, these posttraumatic procedural memories of the body sensations of the trauma may develop a life of their own, expanding to new cues that only vaguely resemble the true memories of the traumatic experience. This process represents negative neuroplasticity. It is due to a process called *neurosensitization*, also known as *kindling*.

Kindling is the name given to a process discovered by chance in the 1960s when neuroscience researchers were trying to map the brain regions of mice by stimulating specific neuronal centers in the brain and recording in adjacent regions. To their surprise, some of the mice began to develop grand mal seizures. The researchers realized that this was a form of neurosensitization, and they called this process "kindling," the word describing wood that burns especially easily. Exploring this new finding, they discovered that the brain region most likely to kindle with repetitive stimulation was our old friend the amygdala. As the diagnosis of PTSD was established in the 1990s, the mental health field discovered the tendency for PTSD victims to actually become worse with time. This deterioration seemed to be primarily due to the increase in the number and intensity of environmental and internal cues that brought on the primary PTSD symptom of arousal and fear. Mental health researchers concluded that this spread of traumatic triggers represented the phenomenon of kindling, a condition that explains many of the seemingly unrelated symptoms of PTSD, the tendency for it to get worse, and especially the tendency for it to change, with the appearance of new symptoms with the passage of time.

The process goes like this:

1. Procedural memories, both of the internal body and external world, are stored in the brain's survival memory bank through the process of fear conditioning.
2. Past memories may be triggered by internal or external cues, and are perceived as being present in the moment.
3. Recurrent unconscious triggering of memories leads to irradiation, or kindling.
4. Repetitive sympathetic autonomic input leads to cyclical autonomic dysregulation—the exaggerated swings between intense sympathetic and parasympathetic states that typify trauma.

With the passage of time, the symptoms of trauma victims change and assume different faces. The exaggerated startle/hyperarousal symptoms may diminish somewhat, and symptoms of depression, withdrawal, avoidance of social contact, and physical collapse may worsen. Somatic symptoms, often involving the gut, the heart, and chronic pain, may appear. Visceral/dissociative/freeze symptoms may become dominant, although with exposure to traumatic cues, hyperarousal may still be profound. The extreme parasympathetic-sympathetic cycling may predominate.

Homeostasis Disrupted:
Abnormal Autonomic Cycling

Recall my discussion of the sine wave in Key 3—the cyclical basis for the function of much of our planet as well as our body. The autonomic nervous system operates on this principal, and the optimal, measured, and well-regulated cycling of that system is called *homeostasis*. But the human condition, the earth, the planets, and the universe are anything but constant and predictable. Any process that is evolving or changing because of unpredictable influences is going to present a challenge to homeostasis, be it a planetary system or the human brain. Waves are not limited to the rhythmic, hypnotic lapping of water on the beaches of

Hawaii—they can become the irregular crashing of waves of different sizes based on a storm at sea hundreds of miles away. They can become the sudden, unpredictable monster of a tsunami, generated by a distant underwater earthquake. The universe, the earth, and the human autonomic nervous system are all subject to the disruption of homeostasis by often unpredictable physical influences.

In mammals, homeostasis involves cycling between sympathetic and parasympathetic dominance, within controlled limits. The peak intensity of each autonomic state is relatively mild, and well within the limits of comfort and the safety of the organ systems of the body. Some researchers have postulated that sustained homeostasis may prevent many disease states. Restoring homeostasis might well be equated with providing an environment for healing. You'll recall that homeostasis is associated with the optimal control of the autonomic nervous system by the ventral vagal nucleus, and can be measured by optimal heart rate variability (the variation in heart rate with inhalation and exhalation; see Key 3).

With regard to the mammalian autonomic nervous system, many researchers believe that repetitive or excessive stimulation of either the sympathetic or parasympathetic arm of the sine wave will result in an increasing intensity and degree of oscillation of the system *to the extremes of its physiological tolerance.* In other words, let's say that persistent and profound arousal is triggered by repetitive exposure to traumatic procedural memory cues. The returning war veteran will be unable to tolerate the normal noises of a city—the honking of taxis, the backfire of a car, the blowing of a police whistle. The rape victim will panic if bumped from behind, when viewing threatening images on television, or upon seeing certain facial expressions within a crowd. These cues kick off the sympathetic nervous system by stimulating the amygdala, but they also cause increased autonomic cycling in *both* directions. This means that deeply pathological parasympathetic freeze states can be activated *along with* the intrinsic sympathetic arousal stimulation. The war veteran may startle at the sound of a car backfiring, but also may "space out" and go numb during an argument with his spouse. The rape victim may panic at cues of the assault but also may dissociate and become unresponsive during sexual foreplay with her husband. One can see how dangerous this might be. One can also see how confusing this would appear to the treating therapist or physician attempting to deal with a single, one-state disease or condition. This is also why the intrinsically bipolar state of brain/autonomic function in trauma is hard to pin down and associate with a definite diagnosis.

Psychological diagnoses for categories of mental illness are based on criteria developed by learned members of the field of mental illness and are presented in the *Diagnostic and Statistical Manual of Mental Disorders, Fourth Edition (DSM-IV)*. This manual is currently in the process of being revised as the *DSM-V*. The fourth edition was published in 1994, after the Vietnam War, when hundreds of soldiers returned with disabling and quite consistent emotional symptoms. These symptoms were given the new diagnosis of posttraumatic stress disorder (PTSD). Study of these soldiers revealed that these symptoms were roughly representative of three definable emotional states. The first was abnormal manifestations of *arousal*, including exaggerated startle response, hypervigilance, sleep disturbance, and irritability—all clearly due to an exaggerated sympathetic state. The soldiers also had abnormalities of their systems of *memory*, including flashbacks of distressing events, nightmares, and exaggerated arousal with exposure to any cues of their traumatic events. And finally, they had symptoms of *avoidance*, including amnesia for traumatic events, avoidance of activities reminiscent of these events, detachment and estrangement from others, and numbing of emotions. One can see why this varied set of symptoms is hard to pin down to a single model of brain physiology.

However, if one looks closely, the primary symptoms of PTSD reflect the autonomic and procedural-memory-based malfunction of the limbic, emotional brain in trauma. Cue-related sympathetic arousal via the amygdala, and parasympathetic avoidance/freeze via the dorsal vagal nucleus, are alternating in an exaggerated fashion that reflects the abnormal autonomic cycling that I've been discussing. Trauma indeed is characterized by the disruption of homeostasis. It's a disease of the brain and, as we'll see, of the body's essential systems.

The Tyranny of the Dorsal Vagus: Sustained Freeze/Dissociation

The mental health field has recognized for some time that the major symptoms of victims of life trauma tend to change over the passage of time. Although symptoms of arousal—anxiety, panic attacks, nightmares, flashbacks, exaggerated startle—do persist, they tend to diminish in frequency and intensity. Unfortunately, this is not necessarily part of the healing process. Trauma victims often begin to isolate themselves socially and emotionally, and retreat into patterns of behavior that avoid any situations that might contain cues related to their trauma history. Emotional numbing and clinical depression are prominent. Trauma victims may develop amnesia not only for events of the trauma but also for portions of their own autobiographical past. Many experience a loss of sense of self and the inability to sense their future. Multiple physical problems, especially bowel complaints, fatigue, and chronic widespread pain (referred to as somatization disorders), often develop. Trauma victims also tend to experience cognitive problems, especially involving short-term memory, concentration, and attention. Trauma develops into many of the symptoms that define dissociation.

I've already related the freeze response to the perceptual state of dissociation (Key 3). So let's look at what types of perceptions can be identified as examples of the state of dissociation. *Depersonalization*, or the out-of-body experience, is one example. You've probably heard of critically injured patients experiencing the perception of looking down on themselves, as if out of their body, as the nurses and doctors tried to revive them. So-called near-death experiences may represent this phenomenon. I've had several patients describe having this experience during a motor vehicle accident. Other dissociative experiences include *derealization*, experienced as déjà vu (the sense that an event has occurred before) or jamais vu (in which the familiar looks strange). *Distorted time perception*, in which a segment of time seems to slow down drastically (like "my life passed before my eyes"), may occur. Dissociation may also be characterized by loss of memory for an event, and memory is particularly impaired in dissociative disorders. *Fugue states* are characterized by prolonged periods of amnesia, often associated with bizarre and even violent behavior for which the person subsequently has no memory. Finally, parts of the body may become paralyzed, clumsy, or anesthetic, a condition called *conversion disorder*, or hysteria. Although this diagnosis has been classified as a somatization disorder in the *DSM-IV*, it actually is a form of dissociation, and will be discussed in Key 7.

Even though these altered states of perception are examples of what one may experience when one is in a state of dissociation, they are really only pieces of the puzzle. The freeze response is clearly driven by the dorsal vagus, but it is associated with dramatic changes throughout the brain, including the limbic brain and all regions of the cerebral cortex. So it's not surprising that large areas of the cerebral cortex may be "off line," or non-functioning, during a dissociative state, probably correlating with the list of altered states of consciousness I just mentioned. And because the autonomic nervous system is very unstable in the freeze, it's also possible that arousal and even sympathetic states may emerge in dissociation. A state of mindless "cold-blooded killing" has been described in soldiers exposed to prolonged, violent combat.

These soldiers assume a "berserker" state during which they pursue violent combat without concern for their own safety, killing everyone in sight in a blank, emotionless state that clearly is dissociative. Whatever its brain-based composition, freeze/dissociation is clearly a well-defined state of altered consciousness with distinctive features.

Remember that these types of memories are supposed to be stored for future reference in order to enhance our survival skills, but they are distorted and intrinsically false because the threat is over. These memories relate to all of the body-based information from a traumatic event that was never fully resolved as being "over and done." And remember that such memories tend to be brought to the surface by cues, or new events that are similar to the old, unresolved trauma.

These somatic memories include autonomic visceral "feelings," somatic sensory messages from any of the body's sense organs, and declarative memories of the trauma that are linked to the emotion of the event. Also recall that, in the freeze response, endorphins are released, so that the capsule of procedural memories is associated with a pervasive sense of numbing of physical sensations and an altered state of awareness. So if you are exposed to something in your environment that provides an intense enough cue to an old trauma, for the moment you will be back in that old state of helplessness, with all of its associated numbing, visceral feelings, body sensations, and altered thoughts. The tendency for recurrent freezing in the face of danger is the hallmark of late, or complex, trauma, which is clearly a syndrome of dissociation. And the dorsal vagal nucleus is the tyrant directing and propelling the show.

Like everything else, trauma can be huge and overwhelming or so subtle that we hardly notice it. The only requirement is that there be a threat involved, and that we have no control over it—that we are helpless to solve it. In other words, even though we don't normally think of a fight with our spouse, for example, as being traumatic, if we have no solution to the problem and feel helpless in the face of what we interpret as a "life threat," that fight could be defined as trauma. And such trauma, whether big or small, is generally accompanied by intrusive thoughts that are difficult to shake.

Exercise

Try to remember a recent situation when you were facing a very specific stress in your life—like a broken relationship, a fight with your signifi-

*cant other, a confrontation at work, or the sudden decline in your 401(k)
as the stock market tanked. Think back to how you physically felt in your
body, what the common theme of your thoughts was, how well (or badly)
you slept, and what unpleasant physical sensations you experienced. Did
you feel in control, or relatively helpless? Was there anger there or just a
touch of anxiety or panic? Did you have any bowel symptoms (bloating,
indigestion, cramps), heartburn, or palpitations of your heart? Did you
have trouble sleeping, especially awakening with racing thoughts that
repeated and couldn't be shut down? Did thinking about these things
during this exercise bring up any of the same symptoms and "feelings" in
your body?*

All of these common symptoms are typical of the effect of "little
traumas" in our lives—conflicted events over which we had no control,
leading to a mixture of arousal/freeze states. The phenomenon is characterized by chronic arousal, sleep disturbance, obsessive persistence,
distraction, and inattentiveness. Sometimes there are even somatic sensations, most commonly myofascial pain around the neck, bruxing
(grinding the teeth), bowel symptoms, and fatigue. What one is dealing
with is a relatively small but well-defined "dissociation capsule" that
keeps interrupting one's present moment and clouding one's mind.
Stress in the face of helplessness becomes trauma, as far as the brain is
concerned.

Endnote

Stress is part of the universal human experience. The basic act of survival on this planet automatically exposes us to stress in many forms.
Some people maintain that a healthy amount of stress—"eustress"—is
actually good for us, bringing on line parts of our autonomic and hormonal response that ultimately make us more adaptive. But stress alone,
involving the hormone cortisol, can adversely affect the brain itself, actually relatively selectively injuring parts of the brain, primarily the neurons of the hippocampus. And in the long run, stress has significant
damaging effects on systems of the body, which I will discuss in Key 7.

Stress and trauma have many features in common but have a very
specific interface based on one's ability to control the situation causing
the stress. Trauma, a life threat in the face of helplessness, ultimately
has a very different neurophysiology than stress, and it affects the brain
and body in many different ways. Trauma has its roots in an unresolved

fight/flight/freeze response, involves the arousal centers of the brain, and profoundly affects autonomic homeostasis. As such, it also profoundly affects the body, but in ways that are variable and hard to measure and therefore create problems for the very linear allopathic physician's mind. In Key 7, I'll explore those problems and that dilemma as well.

Trauma is also a syndrome of the corruption of memory with regard to its relationship to time. Its roots lie in the freeze response, and whether the person is able to complete the fight/flight/freeze process by "discharging," thereby erasing unwanted and now irrelevant somatic procedural memories of the event. If this process is thwarted, traumatic procedural memories will persist and become incorporated into "capsules" of memory, associated with dissociative features of the freeze. These will then recur in the face of internal and external cues related to the unresolved trauma, perpetuating and even enhancing the resulting dysfunctional autonomic cycling and dissociation. The process of neurosensitization, or kindling—when conditioned procedural memory cues spread to similar memories and experiences—ensures that trauma is a gift that just keeps on giving. The good news is that our increasing understanding of the brain-based nature of traumatic conditioning affords us a beacon of light as we seek brain-based means of combating the abnormal neurophysiology of trauma.

THE BODY IN STRESS AND TRAUMA

By this time, you've no doubt caught on to the fact that the brain and the body are parts of a common interactive system. Any outside stimulus or input to the brain must first be registered by the sensory organ systems of the body, and the brain relies on the body to provide all information having to do with function in general, not just survival. What's happening in the body continuously changes the brain. The flip side of this relationship is that the brain, in response, also directs and changes the body. Learning of a motor skill by the brain is dependent on the body's ability to adapt and respond to feedback messages from the brain that direct the somatic musculature. The muscles of the viscera—the organs of the chest and abdomen—also operate through messages from the autonomic nervous system that are generated by the brain, while the sensory messages from these visceral organs inform the brain about one's emotional well-being. The relative health of the brain depends on the health of the body, and vice versa. If trauma has adversely affected either one, you've got to find a means of healing that incorporates both brain and body. You can't fix one without fixing the other.

We've seen how stress and trauma place their own unique imprint on brain function. The spectrum of negative life experiences directly affects how the brain functions, and in some cases actually produces negative physical changes, such as the loss of neurons in the hippocampus through the effects of cortisol, the stress hormone. Stress and trauma can "damage" the brain. It should come as no surprise, then, that abnormal ways that the brain functions in stress and trauma might also "damage" the body. This particular concept has been around for quite a while in the medical field, giving rise to what we now call mind-body medicine, complementary medicine, and in some cases, alternative medicine. The therapeutic approaches employed by this field of practice often incorporate techniques derived from the practice of medicine in the Far East. Examples include meditation, acupuncture, herbs, massage, Qigong, and tai chi, as well as ayurvedic medicine and yoga from India. Most of these practices seek to balance the mind, body, and spirit as a means of preventing and healing disease. This concept certainly has appeal if the primary negative effects on the body in stress and trauma are at least in part due to a disruption in homeostasis, which intrinsically implies a disruption of balance and regulation of brain and body.

There's a dilemma that Western medicine seems to have in dealing with diseases related to brain function, especially alterations in homeostasis. Allopathic, or Western, medicine depends to a significant degree on measurements of the body's chemical/physiological state at a fixed point in time. X rays, scans, microscopic images, blood tests, and so on represent a picture of the body frozen in the moment of the test. One can monitor a person's heart rate, blood pressure, blood-oxygen level, and brain waves for a longer period of time, but this is costly and only gives a brief picture of what we might call the state of homeostasis. Homeostatic disruption almost by definition is associated with emotional disruption and distress. This emotional component often leads the allopathic physician to designate the medical syndromes of trauma as "psychosomatic" diseases, with an emotional and not a physical cause. I think a more accurate term would be *"neurosomatic"* diseases, as these disorders are related to abnormalities in the balanced function of the brain and autonomic nervous system. Although the abnormal body states in trauma are hard to pin down with tests, they still are quite real and definitely are "physical." And this dilemma of a changing, unstable state of abnormal physiology and its symptoms is primarily what we'll be dealing with in considering the body in stress and trauma.

In this Key, I'll review in more detail the effect of cortisol on many of the body's systems, a syndrome Hans Selye called the "general adaptation syndrome," or GAS. The GAS primarily describes what have been called the diseases of stress. We'll also be dealing with a number of diseases and medical syndromes that are prevalent in victims of life trauma but depart from the illness of the GAS. The medical syndromes that I relate specifically to trauma reflect the alterations in brain function that occur in trauma. These include "false" body-based procedural memories, persistence of dissociative freeze states, and neurosensitization, or kindling. Obviously many of these syndromes of trauma represent disorders of regulation of the autonomic nervous system, and therefore involve the visceral organs. I'll also be exploring syndromes and diseases that reflect the frozen somatic procedural memory that characterizes the brain in trauma. This produces not only stuck emotions but also body states reflecting how the brain/body tried to protect itself in trauma. These body states are now frozen as "false" implicit memories—false because they represent memories for an event in the past that is perceived as still being in the present. Many posttraumatic body disorders reflect the kindled, sensitized nature of the brain, leading predictably to syndromes of hypersensitivity to many sensory stimuli. These sensitization disorders, which I call syndromes of kindling, may involve one or more of the body senses. And many trauma syndromes reflect the process of dissociation, or cutting off from awareness, of regions and parts of the somatosensory body that tried but failed to protect the trauma victim.

Cortisol and the Diseases of Stress: The Price of Adaptation

In Key 6 we established a base for understanding the concept of stress. Stress basically demands that the brain and body *adapt* to a *stressor*—an event or experience that disrupts homeostasis but is not sufficient to trigger the full-blown fight/flight response. There's an element of arousal in this process, though not as extreme as that in the fight/flight response, and the amygdala is mildly activated when the brain senses messages that imply even a subtle threat. There is a continuum between stress and trauma that is mainly defined by the degree of helplessness the person is experiencing. In fact, the escalation of a stressor to actually being a life threat is entirely possible. But if the stressor continues without ever becoming a life threat, the brain takes a different pathway than it does in trauma to adapt. This pathway is basically the same as that discussed in Key 3 when I talked about the sympathetic nervous system and its relationship to the hypothalamic-pituitary-adrenal (HPA) axis. The HPA axis is the origin of the hormonal response by the body's endocrine system to prepare the body to adapt to a stressor as long as it persists. The end result is the release of cortisol from the adrenal cortex, or outer layer of the adrenal gland.

As you'll recall, cortisol damages the neurons of the hippocampus and can contribute to memory and cognitive problems in trauma victims. In large amounts, it may also affect the cerebral cortex, producing arousal, vigilance, delusions, anxiety, rage, and even psychosis. As long as the stressor remains present, cortisol will remain elevated in order to help the body deal with the ongoing, low-grade threat. This state of threat will result in the gradual development of the GAS. Helping us maintain vigilance in the face of low-grade threat, the GAS state of autonomic tuning promotes the ability of our heart and circulatory system to deal with increased physical demands and our level of blood glucose to meet the increased caloric energy demands of the body and especially the brain. In the relatively short term, it promotes survival, but in the longer term it literally causes a breakdown of the body.

Cortisol also acts as a modulator of the immune system. In high amounts, it suppresses the immune system. In the early days of organ transplantation, chemicals related to cortisol were used to suppress the immune system to prevent organ rejection. Cortisol-related drugs have also been used in autoimmune diseases, such as rheumatoid arthritis, lupus, and multiple sclerosis. Autoimmune diseases are inflammatory in nature, and cortisol also suppresses inflammation. But improvement in the autoimmune diseases with cortisol is associated with the destructive effects of the GAS. Suppression of the immune system unfortunately also makes the person more prone to what are called "opportunistic" infections by bacteria and viruses that aren't normally very infectious. If taken for a lengthy period of time, cortisol also can contribute to the development of unusual forms of cancer that are generally held in check by the immune system. In many ways, prolonged exposure to cortisol leaves the person subject to many of the tumors and infections seen in the immune deficiency caused by the AIDS virus. As a result, during prolonged stress, persons are vulnerable to the development of viral diseases. That's why cold sores are common under stress.

Cortisol also causes the kidneys to reduce their excretion of salt in the urine. Retaining salt causes blood volume to increase, an important piece of survival insurance in case the threat becomes physical and the person experiences injuries causing a loss of blood. Increased blood volume also guarantees the brain's access to circulation. Both of these effects are adaptive measures for dealing with stress *in the short term*. Cortisol also raises blood pressure, during both exertion and rest, and increases baseline pulse rate, both of which ensure maximal blood flow to the brain. It causes a significant increase in blood glucose levels. The brain counts solely on glucose as a source of energy. Increased vigilance, glucose, blood pressure, pulse, and blood volume help provide support for blood circulation and optimal oxygen and nutrients for brain function—in the short term.

But cortisol also causes an increase in serum cholesterol and other lipids. It causes an increase in secretion of stomach acid. You are probably beginning to see the price exerted by the adaptive GAS. Elevated blood pressure may contribute to sustained hypertension and stroke.

Sustained elevated blood sugar may trigger clinical diabetes. Elevated blood lipids may lead to atherosclerosis and coronary artery disease. Immune suppression may lead to opportunistic infections and conceivably cancer. Elevated stomach-acid secretion may lead to peptic ulcers. Increased vigilance can lead to mental disorders, especially mania and psychosis.

Finally, cortisol in the long run is *catabolic*—it breaks down and changes tissues. It causes wasting of muscles, increased fat deposition about the abdomen, osteoporosis, swelling of the face, and the masculine effects of acne and increased facial hair growth in both genders. Many of these conditions have been called "the diseases of stress," and, in fact, this is partly true. During the early stages of recovery from serious injuries, many of my rehabilitation patients manifested some of these conditions, especially hypertension, acne, cold sores, weight gain, and hypervigilance. Usually these conditions spontaneously subside with time. But if prolonged, the adaptive GAS comes at considerable cost to the brain and body.

Unfortunately the burden of the GAS may not always subside, progressing instead to the diseases and syndromes of trauma. The element of helplessness in an ongoing stressful situation may grow with the passage of time. The burden of financial loss, litigation, impairment of human relationships, and increasing social isolation may cause a shift in brain and body physiology. In this context, a significant number of my injured patients went on to develop what I've called the diseases of trauma, syndromes increasingly at the parasympathetic end of the spectrum of autonomic dysfunction.

The Vagal Freeze and the Viscera: The Tempest in the Heart and Gut

You'll recall that the freeze response is basically governed by the *dorsal vagal nucleus*, the cluster of neurons in the upper medulla, or reptilian brain. The dorsal vagus drastically slows the heart and breath rate so reptiles can hibernate or dive under water for long periods without breathing. The dorsal vagal nucleus also governs the digestive process, increasing digestive secretions in the stomach, small intestine, and colon to regulate absorption of nutrients. It also controls contraction of the muscles of these abdominal visceral organs to move the lump of food products down the line, eventually getting rid of waste products of digestion after extracting water by the colon, or large intestine. Beginning with saliva in the mouth, the digestive secretions of each segment of the gut are released to break down the proteins, carbohydrates, and fats in the diet, readying the food for absorption by the small intestine. The last act of digestion controlled by the dorsal vagus is relaxing the anal sphincter, or valve, to promote defecation. Other sphincters between the esophagus, the stomach, the small intestine, and the colon serve to prevent reflux, or backflow, of the digestive products into the previous chamber. The dorsal vagus controls the smooth regulation of these sphincters so they open and close when they're supposed to. The whole process of digestion involves the parasympathetic nervous system, as discussed in Key 3. This vagal function regulates the state of resting and restoring.

In Key 3 I also discussed the role of the dorsal vagus in the freeze response in both reptiles and mammals. Although this function is useful for diving or hibernating reptiles, it puts mammals, which can't tolerate long periods of drastically reduced heart rate and respiration, in peril. Mammals may die from cardiac arrest in a prolonged freeze state. You'll recall that wild rats that died in the freeze state were found to have dilated hearts filled with blood, arrested during the state of relaxation in the heart-beat cycle. Profound dorsal vagal prominence related to the freeze can literally freeze movement of the heart in mammals. It can also lead to a number of well-recognized but puzzling syndromes involving the lungs, heart, and gut. It should be noted that these syndromes often occur together, and they are associated with mood disturbances, including anxiety, depression, sleep disturbance, headache, and backache. In the United States, women constitute approximately two thirds of the population who suffer from these syndromes of the freeze. And all of these syndromes, except perhaps asthma, are more common in the population of patients being treated for trauma, especially those with an increased incidence of childhood trauma. The diseases of the freeze therefore reflect the physical, somatic collapse and paralysis of the freeze response, the overactivity of the glands and muscles of the viscera, and the exaggerated cycling of parasympathetic and sympathetic visceral states.

Fibromyalgia and Chronic Fatigue Syndrome

I consider fibromyalgia and chronic fatigue syndrome (CFS) to be the prototype for diseases of freeze/dissociation. Fibromyalgia is characterized by long-term, body-wide pain and tenderness in the joints, muscles, and tendons. Chronic fatigue syndrome is basically characterized by cycles of physical exhaustion to the point of being bedridden at times. All of the other syndromes of the freeze discussed in this Key are extremely common in fibromyalgia and form part of its spectrum. These include gastroesophageal reflux disease, irritable bowel syndrome, mitral valve prolapse, and multiple chemical sensitivities. Fibromyalgia and CFS occur together most of the time but may also occur independently.

Fibromyalgia may begin at any age, but it usually occurs in young adulthood, often in the context of a new life trauma. Many of my whiplash patients developed fibromyalgia in the context of recovering from their injury. It is a common syndrome, affecting around 5% of the general population, and is generally placed among the rheumatic disorders. As a result most cases get referred to rheumatologists. The problem with treating fibromyalgia is that the syndrome creates no tissue changes or consistent abnormalities that show up on blood or X-ray tests, leading it to be widely considered a psychosomatic disorder. Allopathic medicine offers no specific effective treatments for it.

A new designation for fibromyalgia is that of "chronic widespread pain," the major complaint of this condition. Other symptoms include diffuse tenderness over specific points or areas on the body, morning stiffness, nonrestorative sleep and daytime fatigue, numbness, tingling, cognitive impairment, hypervigilance, and emotional instability. CFS may occur by itself, but it is frequently allied with fibromyalgia. It is characterized by generalized, often profound fatigue, sometimes to the point of collapse. The remarkable breadth and complexity of fibromyalgia symptoms, and its cyclical nature, strongly suggest a disorder of diffuse autonomic regulation. The symptoms of weakness, collapse, and cognitive impairment mirror the state of freeze/dissociation. The widespread nature of the systems involved suggests an element of early-childhood, perhaps preverbal, trauma. Pain is a major part of fibromyalgia, leading to the latest treatment du jour, a drug called Lyrica, which is basically one of a group of mild anticonvulsants promoted for the treatment of chronic pain.

Asthma

The dorsal vagus causes increase in bronchial mucus secretions and constricts the bronchial tubes in the lungs. This reflects a relative state of rest, when the deep, rapid breathing necessary for the fight/flight response is no longer necessary and the lungs can relax and lubricate the bronchi. But, as with everything else in physiology, any natural state that is taken to an extreme can be pathological and dangerous. In the case of asthma, this is reflected in wheezing and cough. The constriction of the bronchi can be severe enough to be life-threatening. Normal constriction of the bronchial tubes and increased secretions in the resting state can, in the deep and persistent freeze state, become asthma. Asthma as a disease is one that closely reflects the unresolved physiology of the freeze response.

Asthma is somewhat unique among the syndromes discussed in this Key. As you'll see, many of the other syndromes of the freeze often occur together, seldom occur in early childhood, and have prominent emotional symptoms. Asthma, on the other hand, often is a syndrome of early childhood. It frequently occurs before or in the absence of a history of personal trauma or abuse, although asthma attacks *are* commonly precipitated by highly emotional events. There is anecdotal evidence of increased incidence of birth trauma or other negative neonatal factors in asthma, but no solid evidence. I would suggest that asthma may reflect preverbal, or even intrauterine, trauma. We do know that the emotional state of the mother during pregnancy may have profound effects on the fetus, probably based on increased maternal cortisol levels that are passed on to the fetus through the placenta. In fact, emotional distress in the mother during pregnancy appears to be related to hippocampal atrophy as well as reduced birth weight in the infant. But the posttraumatic nature of asthma based on the physiology of the freeze must still be considered speculative.

Mitral Valve Prolapse

The dorsal vagus lessens the rate and strength of heart contractions, reducing blood pressure and blood flow in the body. One result is an arrhythmia, or irregular heart beat. The heart also has valves, analogous to the sphincters in the gut, that prevent reflux of blood from one chamber to another. The left side of the heart contains the mitral valve, preventing reflux of blood from the left ventricle back into the left atrium. In trauma, the unstable physiology of the freeze results in a loss of synchrony between these two chambers, resulting in prolapse, or excessive backward extension of the mitral valve into the atrium when the ventricle contracts. The person with mitral valve prolapse (also known as *dysautonomia*) experiences palpitations, or a fluttering sensation in the chest, sometimes associated with a sense of panic. The irregular and exaggerated autonomic cycling of trauma triggers a sympathetic response with arousal, along with an alteration of the normal heart rhythm. The name *dysautonomia* reflects both the parasympathetic state of the freeze, with cardiac arrhythmias, and the underlying abnormal autonomic cycling, with sympathetically based arousal and panic. Although imaging studies demonstrate the abnormal prolapse of the mitral valve, there are no other anatomical explanations for this syndrome. As noted, it is commonly associated with all of the other freeze syndromes.

Gastroesophageal Reflux Disease

As I've implied, the freeze response is a dorsal vagal state, but because of autonomic cycling, there is also a sympathetic component to the syndromes associated with it. One must remember that the freeze response is always triggered by arousal related to some old posttraumatic cue, followed by a rapid descent into the freeze state. So all of these syndromes are also characterized by a disruption of synchrony. Gastroesophageal reflux disease (GERD) is similar to mitral valve prolapse, except that the reflux occurs between the stomach and the esophagus in GERD. The asynchronous contraction of stomach and esophagus prevents the valve from performing its function, resulting in reflux of gastric acid into the esophagus. The stomach lining contains chemicals that neutralize excessive acid, but the esophagus does not. As a result the acid literally "burns" the esophageal lining, resulting in what we call "heartburn" or "acid indigestion." An extremely common condition, GERD is allegedly related to stress but actually more linked to traumatic stress and the dorsal vagus/freeze state. The syndrome tends to occur in conditions of approach/avoidance conflict, with its implications of helplessness and therefore the freeze. The relentless marketing of stomach-acid-inhibitor drugs on television suggests how common GERD is in our society. It is one of the most common complaints of soldiers returning from Iraq and Afghanistan, and it is ubiquitous in those with PTSD.

Irritable Bowel Syndrome

Irritable bowel syndrome (IBS) is another cyclical bowel syndrome that is almost as common as GERD. It affects both the small and large intestines, leading to alternating constipation and diarrhea, with cramping abdominal pain, bloating and gassiness, and increased mucous in the stools. The alternating parasympathetic/sympathetic nature of these symptoms certainly suggests exaggerated autonomic cycling. IBS usually occurs in people under the age of 40. As with GERD, many physicians relate IBS to stress, but once again, it is a separate syndrome from those associated with Selye's GAS.

The symptoms of IBS blend with those associated with lactose and gluten intolerance, and it's often difficult to separate the two. In gluten intolerance, the genetic trait may progress to the more severe celiac disease, especially in the face of stress or trauma. This isn't surprising given the tendency for kindling, or neurosensitization, to occur in victims of trauma. Kindling in these posttraumatic cases clearly can amplify the symptoms of bona fide gluten intolerance and cause this to progress to full blown IBS and ultimately celiac disease. This is another example of negative neuroplasticity, as discussed in Key 5.

Syndromes of Kindling

Because of the sensitized wiring of circuits in the brain, people who've experienced life trauma are easily sensitized to virtually any sensory input. Their brains are kindled to respond to sensory input as representing threat. Other states that reflect this sensitized brain wiring include hypervigilance and exaggerated startle (sympathetic), often alternating with fogginess, "spacing out," and dissociation (parasympathetic). Virtually any sense can be kindled, but smell is the most sensitive to kindling. In mammals it is the main sense used for detection of threat, although its function has atrophied in the urbanized human. Nevertheless, syndromes such as multiple chemical sensitivities, multiple environmental allergies, and sick building syndrome reflect the sensitivity of smell to kindling. All of these conditions are valid and definitely physiological. They are not based on the imagination of the person suffering from them. These people's brain physiology is actively engaging the process of sensory hypersensitivity in an effort to protect them.

Perhaps the prototype syndrome of kindling is the fairly recent diagnostic designation of "sensory processing disorder" (SPD). This is a theoretical model for the inherent difficulty in detecting, modulating, and interpreting all of the avenues of sensory input in some children. Children with SPD experience a wide range of abnormal perceptions and responses to ordinary body sensations. These responses may be oversensitive (kindling), or undersensitive (dissociation), and may involve any of the body sensory experiences: smell, vision, hearing, taste, vestibular sensation, touch, and proprioception. Such children may seek out, or avoid, any of these sensations. Most children with SPD will also show symptoms of attention deficit disorder (ADD). The disorder is related to negative early childhood experiences, including prenatal or birth trauma, attachment disorder, developmental childhood trauma and abuse, and even the autism spectrum. Exaggerated (sympathetic) or dulled (parasympathetic) sensitivity to any or all of the primary sensations may be present in these cases.

All of these syndromes of kindling are associated with abnormal autonomic regulation and are improved with techniques designed to promote homeostasis. Many of these techniques have been devised by the occupational therapy community. SPD in childhood can be diminished by treatment, but it generally persists into adult life, probably reflecting many of the syndromes of kindling that we've discussed.

All of the smell-based sensitization syndromes are basically products of an overactive sympathetic arousal response system. Recall that the olfactory nerve accesses the amygdala without going through the "filter" of the thalamus. The immediate response is arousal/anxiety triggered by the sensitized amygdala. Once the sequence of arousal/fear has been initiated, the intensity of autonomic cycling accelerates to the point of multiple physical symptoms, both sympathetic (fear, terror, tremor) and parasympathetic (nausea, weakness, cramps, trouble breathing). Symptoms reflect the intensity of the autonomic state driving them. And the detection of minute olfactory messages is quite valid. I sincerely believe that the kindled, environmentally sensitive person is able to detect the smell of tobacco in the house next door, or perfume coming from someone in a crowd across the room.

Sensitivity to light or visual cues can be related to the intensity of the light, the flickering of 60-cycle fluorescent lights, or the speed of movement of the visual object. Sensitivity to sounds may be due to the volume, the dissonance, or, in music, to the pitch, rapidity, intensity, or sequence of chords. The "white noise" of a vaporizer, hypnotic to many, can suddenly become irritating and intolerable to the kindled individual. Proprioceptive and vestibular sensitivity may be manifested by simple dizziness, but also by positional vertigo with minimal head movement and bouts of imbalance. The diagnosis in this case often is benign positional vertigo. Disembarkment syndrome is related to the long-term perpetuation of the feeling of instability and balance impairment one feels after getting off a boat. In most people, this feeling disappears in minutes, but it may persist indefinitely in the kindled individual.

Hypersensitivity to rough fabrics such as wool, or to the label in a collar, may also be a form of kindling. The kindled lover may be able to tolerate firm touch but not the caress of his or her lover.

There also may be an element of suggestibility in sensitization disorders, a trait that has been called "effort after meaning." Sensitivity to the electrical field around power lines, or exposure to subclinical levels of carbon monoxide, may produce dramatic physical syndromes in the sensitized person but not in other members of the family. As I mentioned earlier, many people suffer from lactose and gluten intolerance on a genetic basis, and often are able to manage this easily with dietary measures. However, the kindled individual with a history of trauma may also experience worsening of the gastrointestinal symptoms in these sensitivities. They may spread to involve other related food groups and progress to full-blown IBS, especially in the context of new life trauma or threat. But the effect of suggestibility is neither a psychosomatic phenomenon nor an issue of secondary gain or reward. The pathological alteration in the person's physiology is perfectly real. The perception of threat itself will alter the brain of the sensitized individual and create the visceral, physical symptom via the unstable autonomic nervous system.

Sensorimotor Syndromes and Chronic Pain: "The Gain in Pain Lies Mainly in the Brain"

I've talked a great deal about sensorimotor procedural memory, first as a method for learning complex motor skills, and second as a way of learning survival skills though unconscious classical conditioning. I've also talked about how, in trauma, body-based memories are stored as being in the present—even though the traumatic event is in the past—through the imprinting in memory of the sensory and motor patterns of the undischarged freeze response. This storage of "false" body memories plagues the trauma survivor in the form of intrusive memories, or flashbacks. These posttraumatic memories contain not only the explicit, declarative content and meaning of the event, but also the sensory experiences—smells, images, sounds, and body sensations that emerge in the form of sensory symptoms or unconscious movements, such as tics.

But one doesn't need to have a specific flashback memory for these unconscious sensations and incomplete movement patterns to emerge under certain circumstances. Like everything in the brain and body in trauma, the emergence of memories, sensations, or emotions associated with the trauma can be prompted by *cues*. These can be both internal (in the body, in memories of other events similar to the trauma) or external (actual, ambient experiences from our everyday life environment). When we experience such cues, they often go completely unnoticed. For example, one of my patients reported feeling inexplicably uncomfortable in the presence of a therapist she had been referred to, despite the therapist's personable demeanor. When I asked the patient how she would describe the therapist, she thought about it and suddenly flushed. She had recalled that the therapist used red nail polish, a favorite of her grandmother who had abused her.

In complex and repeated trauma, a person's environment may literally be packed with stimuli related in some way to old traumatic experiences. It's no wonder that trauma victims often suffer from agoraphobia —the fear of spaces, crowds, or any environment with many stimuli. These stimuli often trigger not only panic attacks but also many somatic complaints. Many of these somatic symptoms were just discussed in syndromes of the freeze and are predominantly visceral and autonomic symptoms. But many somatic complaints, particularly pain, stiffness, and muscular problems, are also related to triggers from environmental cues.

Possibly the most common source of chronic discomfort seen in doctor's offices, myofascial pain is stiffness and chronic pain mainly experienced in the spinal muscles, and especially in the neck and low back. It is the cause for what we call "tension headaches." It's usually more severe on one side than the other, and frequently is very specific and localized to a particular muscle group. The most common muscle involved is the levator scapulae, running from the middle region of the neck down to the scapula, or shoulder blade. Its primary function is to elevate the scapula and to pull the neck and shoulder forward. Another common muscle is the masseter, which attaches the lower jaw to the skull and tightens when we clench our teeth. In the lower spine, the primary muscle usually involved is the iliopsoas, a complex muscle that runs from the mid-lumbar spine down to the inside of the pelvis and then down to the femur, or thigh bone. It pulls the femur up to the abdomen, and pulls the lower spine down toward the pelvis, hyperextending it. The end result of all these muscles contracting at the same time replicates the posture of the "startle response." When we hear a sudden loud noise, we "flinch," pulling our neck down, our shoulders up, our arms forward across our body, our jaws open, and our legs up against the abdomen. All of these muscles susceptible to myofascial pain are instinctually wired for self-protection and survival. They protect the vulnerable body areas (throat and abdomen) that a predator will attack. The body's response to a threat is to contract these muscles automatically.

Myofascial pain, in other words, is regional spasm of muscles that tried to protect us in a traumatic event but failed to do so because we were helpless, froze, and didn't extinguish the trauma through the freeze discharge. Of course, muscles other than those just mentioned may also be involved. In other words, procedural memory for the use of any muscle group used in self-defense that was unsuccessful will imprint the procedural memory for that physical self-protective movement pattern in our survival brain. In the face of cues to that trauma, or any threat for that matter, our brain will automatically activate those muscle groups that tried and failed to protect us. This results in "nervous tics," tremors, torticollis (compulsive neck turning), or painful spasms, especially in spinal muscles. It will produce strange changes in our body posture, especially the neck-forward, slumped posture of "aging." As we age, our physical bodies and posture basically reflect the burden of our cumulative life trauma, driven there by our unresolved traumatic procedural memory.

This process also relates to the sensory experiences of trauma. All of the varied sensory experiences of an unresolved traumatic event will also be stored along with the motor responses. A prime example of this is the phenomenon of phantom limb pain, which I discussed in detail in Key 5. Procedural memory for the painful sensations accompanying an unresolved traumatic event will be stored just as the complex patterns of the failed muscular act of self-protection were. One doesn't need to have the limb amputated to experience posttraumatic "phantom" pain. In fact, doctors and their patients frequently face the common problem of a specific pain having no explainable cause despite multiple imaging tests. And it may be resistant to all efforts at cure, including medications, nerve blocks, and even spinal surgery for a "ruptured disc." In many cases, that's because the pain indeed is "phantom" pain due to its basis in posttraumatic procedural memory. It's also the type of pain that's eventually considered to be "psychosomatic." Any pain embedded in the brain's procedural memory by trauma will assume the state of phantom pain. As you'll recall, Ramachandran was able to cure phantom limb pain by using a mirror box to effect a behavioral reversal of how the brain perceives the amputated limb. Other behavioral techniques that can cure "phantom pain" will be discussed in Key 8.

Exercise

To illustrate this point, I'd like you to repeat an exercise we did earlier in the book. Not everyone has experienced the types of pain and movement disorders that I've described, but most are familiar with the common "crick in your neck"—the pain or soreness in the levator scapulae muscle that runs from one side of the middle of your neck to the inside tip of your shoulder blade. This is the muscle you often see people massaging when they're taking a class, working at their computer, or attending a lecture or concert. They'll often roll their head around at the same time. Pay attention to this muscle while you do the exercise.

First, put the book down, sit comfortably with your feet on the floor and your arms by your side, and shut your eyes. Do a body scan for any tightness, tension, or discomfort in your muscles. Then reflect on your current life events and find one that is important and unresolved, and that has at least some slight element of conflict, threat, or uncertainty. When you find it, concentrate on the story of that event, particularly those elements that contain any negative energy or where you're not in control of the situation. Focus on the nuances and details of that conflict, its implications, and whatever frustration it generates. After 1 or 2 minutes, do another body scan for any tightness or discomfort.

You may not feel anything specific. But I would predict that some of you will indeed experience a sense of tightness or even discomfort in some region of your body—most likely, in the pesky levator scapulae region. But the discomfort may also occur in some other muscular body region. If so, search your memory bank for some negative life experience that may have involved that muscle group. You may find it. Some of you may actually get a "visceral" response—tightness or cramping in your gut, increased heart rate, a little heartburn, needing to take a deep breath. If any of this occurs, you have experienced the role of unconscious procedural memories in the creation of physical symptoms—symptoms that are quite real.

Of course, *any* sensory message in an unresolved traumatic event—not just pain—may also be stored in procedural memory. In other publications I've written a great deal about how "whiplash syndrome" may represent a broad array of sensory symptoms that reflect procedural memory for all of the sensations experienced in an auto accident. These include impairment of visual focus, positional vertigo (dizziness), ringing in the ears, bouts of nausea, impaired memory and cognition, TMJ (jaw clenching), sleep impairment and chronic fatigue, migraines, balance disturbance, and of course neck and low back pain. All of the basic sensations involved in movement may be stored—vision, hearing, vestibular sense, body proprioception, and patterns of muscular contraction—leading to recurrent replication of these sensations with cues based on procedural memory. A sizeable number of medical articles consider whiplash to be a psychosomatic syndrome. In fact, it's one of many poorly understood physical syndromes that have their basis in the brain physiology of trauma.

Whiplash is somewhat unique as a syndrome of somatic procedural memory, probably because of the complexity of the experience. I've also discussed phantom limb pain as a phenomenon of procedural memory for pain. It's very likely that most of inexplicable chronic pain may well be "phantom"—based on traumatic procedural memory, not ongoing disease of the painful tissues "Failed" back surgery, where the surgery itself was successful but the pain remains unchanged, may be another example. In fact, whenever the physical injury is associated with helplessness, one must consider the possibility that persisting pain may be due to this physiological, not psychosomatic, cause. Helplessness in the injury experience is probably the best predictor of persisting pain. And unfortunately, the rigid requirements for safety, consistency, and accountability demanded of our hospital system may unwittingly sow the seeds of helplessness in patients who enter it.

We know from scientific studies that professional football players and demolition derby drivers occasionally get a temporary sore neck but virtually never get the constellation of symptoms seen in whiplash. The obvious reason is that men who participate in these sports are aggressors/predators, not prey. They are not helpless, and they don't freeze and store procedural memories for the injuries they may suffer. It's no surprise that the same behavioral therapies that cure phantom limb pain may cure the "phantom" constellation of symptoms seen in whiplash.

Somatic Dissociation: Stigmata, Hysteria, and Reflex Sympathetic Dystrophy

I gave you a "teaser" at the end of Key 5 about how using the mirror box to "fool" the brain into perceiving the painful or missing body part as being normal may cure the pain. One can actually extinguish traumatic procedural memory by changing the brain's perception. I presented reflex sympathetic dystrophy (RSD) as being a model of false traumatic

procedural memory. I also introduced the concept of somatic dissociation of a body part that participated in the unsuccessful act of self-
defense, and its effects on the autonomic regulation of that body part.
We will now explore this phenomenon in more breadth and detail.

Many of my patients who had suffered physical injuries were also
traumatized by the violent nature of the experience and had elements
of PTSD. These patients were all basically clumsy, constantly bumping
into door jambs, bruising themselves, stepping off curbs and spraining
ankles, or bumping their heads on kitchen cupboards. They seemed to
have lost touch with their bodies in space. And indeed that's what they
were experiencing—the splitting off from awareness of parts of their
body, primarily those parts that had experienced the sensory messages
of the traumatic event itself. And they had no conscious awareness of
this disconnection. It's a lot like the brain was splitting off that dangerous body part from perception in order to protect itself. The body part
carried the messages of the trauma, and now was being "figuratively"
discarded. The brain literally "shot the messenger."

The more the body part had been involved in perceiving the traumatic event, or attempting to protect the person from it, the more it was
"shut off" from awareness, or dissociated. And that body part or region
at some point became vulnerable to developing abnormal autonomic
changes, including the chronic burning pain of RSD. For example,
one patient had fallen from a ladder, breaking her nose and spraining
both wrists. Whenever she came in for a visit, and we talked about how
she was doing, her nose and both hands became flushed. Similarly,
when the patient of a colleague of mine reexperienced, during a therapy session, the memory of an assault by her husband, a handprint,
fingers toward the ear, blossomed in red on the left side of her face.
When a patient of mine who had been broadsided on the right side of
her car came to see me, she said her hair was growing more slowly on
the right side of her head. Upon inspection, she had bald spots only on
the right side, her right-hand nails were split and broken, and her right
hand was cooler than the left. While recalling a traumatic injury, these
patients developed autonomic changes, some sympathetic, some parasympathetic, in the body parts, or even the region, where they had experienced the event. Those body parts were split off from normal
awareness, and the circulation was altered. I have called this phenomenon *somatic dissociation*. The parasympathetic red spots mapping the
sensory pattern of the traumatic event are a potential prelude for RSD,
and in fact can be called *stigmata*.

Stigmata, of course, are associated with the replication of the wounds of Christ on Thursdays and Fridays, the days of Christ's Passion, in the Catholic Church. Many of the early saints in the Catholic Church experienced stigmata. The stigmata of somatic dissociation have no religious significance, but like religious stigmata, they occur in parts or areas of the body that experienced the sensory messages of a traumatic event. And in a few cases, I have observed such stigmata to progress to the cold, painful, and dystrophic symptoms of RSD in the affected body part. In my own personal case, a severe skiing injury involving a shattered shoulder led to this state. After surgery and unremitting pain, the dressings were removed, and there on the front of my shoulder were three red patches. At the time, I wondered what possibly could have caused them, but then I noted that I was having difficulty feeling the arm and hand, or finding where they actually were without looking for them. My entire arm was clearly dissociated. This rapidly progressed to burning pain, and I realized that I was actually getting RSD! I was experiencing a phenomenon that had been identified and addressed over a century ago in Paris, France. Fortunately I was acquainted with many local therapists who successfully treat RSD with trauma therapy, and in several weeks my pain, stigmata, and symptoms were gone.

The selective dissociation of a region or part of the body has been discussed by Onno van der Hart and his colleagues under the name of "somatoform dissociation," a state that represents what was called "conversion hysteria" in the language of late-19th-century psychiatry and psychology. This condition almost solely affected women, and the study of hysteria mainly took place in Paris. It was characterized by paralysis, bizarre involuntary movement patterns, seizures, blindness, loss of sensation, and a host of other neurological disabilities without any physical explanation. Stigmata in the affected body part often accompanied hysteria. Sigmund Freud, the father of modern psychiatry, studied these women and found that the common feature in their personal history was early sexual abuse. Suffice it to say, the sensorimotor disabilities of these unfortunate women replicated all of the same brain function that leads to the tics, stigmata, loss of awareness of selected body parts, and RSD that I've been describing in this section.

Like Freud's patients, many of my patients with conversion hysteria had suffered severe childhood physical or sexual abuse. Conversion hysteria is quite common in neurological practice—most of the symptoms have to do with neurological deficits. I have found in my patients that the tics, patterns of compulsive abnormal movements, and sensory loss quite accurately reflect those parts of the body that participated in a failed act of self-defense. These movement patterns were held in procedural memory for life, to be resurrected (unfortunately uselessly) under threat, or under cues in the environment of the original trauma.

You'd think that tics, hysterical postures, and movement patterns would be quite common in war veterans. Although they do occur, they are relatively rare in our soldiers returning from Iraq and Afghanistan. For one thing, hysteria is much more common in women, which gives a clue to its rarity among male soldiers from recent wars. This is so perhaps because women are more likely to freeze, or dissociate, than men. Some researchers in behavioral science feel that the freeze response in early hunter-gatherer women and their children enhanced their chances of survival in an attack by another tribe, where fighting or attempting to flee would be fatal. In addition, females and children lack the violence gene that is switched on at puberty in adolescent males.

But in World War I, a syndrome called "shell shock" was rampant in many if its male combatants. At the time, the armed forces, and the psychiatrists treating these men, believed shell shock was a form of malingering, or hysteria—the odd symptoms of this syndrome had not been documented before. The key to this strange departure in behavior from other wars lies in the prolonged period of trench warfare. During artillery bombardments, as the soldiers cowered in the trenches, they were completely helpless to defend themselves. After the bombardments, as the soldiers tried to recover and prepare themselves for battle, a fairly large number of them remained frozen in the mud of the trench, locked in the posture of self-defense. Many of the soldiers never recovered from this posture. They remained physically frozen, blind, deaf, mute, and with numerous tics for the rest of their institutionalized lives. Shell shock and its sensorimotor responses reflected freeze/dissociation in the face of overwhelming helplessness.

So here we have a continuum of symptoms, experiences, and behavior that reflect all of the sensorimotor syndromes of trauma. The freeze "discharge" is a completion of the act of self-defense, and it extinguishes procedural memory of the trauma. When a "discharge" occurs in a patient during psychotherapy, it looks not only like the act of self-defense, but also very much like the patterns of movement in hysteria. Both of these states also reflect the repetitive movement patterns that we call "tics," which also represent incomplete replications of failed muscular acts of self-defense. And, finally, the body parts that take part in tics, shell shock, and hysteria are "dissociated" and vulnerable under further stress to develop the dissociative autonomic syndrome of RSD. You might even call it the tic–somatic experiencing discharge–conversion hysteria–RSD continuum.

Endnote

The spectrum of what can happen to the body in stress and trauma is broad and deep. Under stress, we see a diverse group of changes in many organ, endocrine, and immune-system functions of the body that reflect their exposure to elevated levels of the stress hormone cortisol. This process begins in the arousal systems of the brain, the amygdala and the limbic system, but falls short of the physiology of the fight/flight response. The stress response engages the hypothalamus, pituitary, and adrenal glands. It becomes more an autonomic and endocrine response than an ongoing central nervous system response. The cerebral cortex is basically not involved in the stress response, although the neurons of the hippocampus may be damaged by the relatively elevated cortisol levels. The physical harm to organs and tissues is secondary to elevated cortisol, and includes elevated blood sugar (diabetes), elevated serum lipids (atherosclerosis), elevated stomach acid (peptic ulcers), osteoporosis, elevated blood volume (hypertension), and depressed immune function (opportunistic infections, cancer). These diseases are specific to an individual hormone rather than a locked-in change in the brain, and they depend upon the continued input of stress to the limbic brain by external, environmental influences. They will persist as long as the stress continues. If stress proceeds to helplessness, however, the physiology changes from a cortisol, endocrine reaction to an autonomic/freeze syndrome.

The diseases of trauma are caused by a much more complex fixed change in specific brain functions. They can't be cured by removing an environmental stimulus. They are based on corrupted procedural memory systems by an altered brain. The causes are diverse based on the shifting, unstable state of the brain and autonomic nervous system in trauma. When the freeze response and dissociation are most prominent, one tends to see cyclical extremes of abnormal function in the viscera, characteristics that allopathic medicine tends to call psychosomatic diseases. When sympathetic influences are most pronounced, one will primarily see syndromes of sensitization, or kindling, to one or many body sensory systems and environmental sources, especially smell. And when the somatic body experiences pain, especially related to the musculature, the source is primarily the problem of old, cue-related, unresolved traumatic procedural memory. In extreme cases of trauma with prominent dissociative states, one may also see a combination of pain related to procedural memory along with abnormal regulation of circulation in the affected region of the body.

You must certainly be wondering how we can possibly treat and heal this wide-ranging, complex, incredibly diverse group of diseases and brain/body dysfunctions. Most of you will have already recognized a few, or even many, of these symptoms in yourselves. The traumatic sources for these syndromes are all over the place in our complex, hierarchical, demanding culture. They are driven by our daily work and family interactions and the limits and demands of a pyramidal, trickledown urban culture, with its endless supply of "little traumas" and approach-avoidance stress. The good news is that we now recognize these abnormal states of health, and their basic brain physiology. If some of these diseases related to stress are due to the autonomic regulation in stress, then we need to find means of providing autonomic self-regulation skills. If many of these diseases are related to abnormal, locked-in conditioned procedural memory, we need to develop systems of *fear extinction* to bring these body memories out of the present moment and place them back in the past where they belong. Nothing, of course, is as easy as words might imply. But the tools are there, and they are also the tools that are emerging in using and treating the symptoms of the body in healing trauma. These tools and their principles will be the topic of Key 8.

PART IV

HOW WE CAN REPAIR OUR BRAIN

HEALING YOUR WOUNDED BRAIN AND BODY

How do we even begin to contemplate "fixing" this relatively unknowable, infinitely complex electrochemical/structural system of the brain/body wounded by stress and trauma? We've got an unstable system, cycling out of control, coming and going like a will-o'-the-wisp, presenting itself with myriad symptoms, states, and feelings with no apparent connection to anything that makes sense. No wonder we "feel like we're crazy" when we're in this state, why our spouses and family retreat in despair, why we've forgotten what sleep is like, why we can't keep track of our lives, why every bone in our body aches with an ague (how can we hurt so much when we're completely numb?), and why the doctor always rolls his eyes and turns his head away when we tell him our symptoms. The wound is not only in our body and brain, but also in our very basic sense of self, in our soul, in the core of our being. We have no anticipated future, we can't find any sense of the present, and we're either assaulted by the past or in some strange space suspended in an unknowable time. How could anyone else possibly understand what this unique state of misery is like?

There are hundreds of thousands, perhaps millions, of people in this country who would recognize themselves in the preceding paragraph. And that description only scratches the surface of the suffering in the brain and body of the person experiencing the effects of complex trauma. There are many, many books devoted to helping people understand how to "heal trauma." If they all worked, this book and chapter would not be relevant. Healing the wounded brain/body in trauma is as complex as the wound itself.

As I mentioned earlier, I've found that teaching my patients about how their brains/bodies are functioning—or not functioning—provides them with a degree of power and control over their physical experience. Knowing that their misery is real, explainable, and understandable is a form of empowerment, the antithesis of helplessness. And empowerment is an essential ingredient in any form of therapy.

Throughout this book, I've made an effort to provide a basic understanding of how the brain and body work in concert, often sacrificing
scientific detail in order to make the information relatively accessible.
The same dilemma will apply to my discussion of healing, correcting,
and modulating abnormal trauma-related physiology in the brain and
body. But I will make the case that if we change or heal the brain, the
body will follow. The servosystem begins with the body's sensations but
ends with the brain's executive functions. Although together they form
an integral whole, the brain remains the control center, the source, and
the part of the duo that is corrupted in trauma. It is the brain's normal
integrated and homeostatic physiology that we've got to restore. There
is no "chicken or the egg" dilemma here—if you treat the chicken,
you'll improve the egg.

But that doesn't mean you don't *use* the body in the process of healing. After all, the original sensory messages that contributed to changing the brain in trauma came from the body's sensory organs and warned
the brain in the first place. Those sensory messages, and the procedural
memory related to them, are the basic informational substrate of trauma
in the brain. Even though the body represents these memories in sensory symptoms, abnormal movement patterns, and even deterioration
of body tissue, the physiology of the brain is what drives these changes.
Conversely, we can use the messages of the body once again to change
the way the brain observes and regulates the body's activity. For example, we can extinguish and "cure" the nervous tic by accessing the "felt
sense" of the body to trigger the discharge, or "completion," of the act
of self-defense, which then extinguishes the motor procedural memory
of the tic. Of course, it is the brain that directs this "discharge" and thus
begins to heal itself.

Where these posttraumatic procedural memories are stored, and in
what form, is another important consideration. In general, every traumatic event is associated with stored memories that are varied and
uniquely complex, and are not part of a seamless, connected story.
Each of the sensorimotor body states reflects the precisely specific sensory elements of the traumatic experience. Each traumatic experience
is by nature quite unique, with several exceptions. If a traumatic act is
purposely repeated by the perpetrator, such as in the case of incest, the
memories, reflecting a similar, repeated event, will be relatively precise
and therefore very powerful. But whatever the source, every life trauma
will have its own specific memories, triggered by their own specific
cues. What I am describing is a *state* composed of consistently reproducible procedural memories. These memories involve body sensa-

tions, visceral feelings, autonomic states (also with their own feelings), emotions, and patterns of unconscious self-protective muscle contractions. Because these memories are linked to emotion, traumatic cues will also be associated with declarative memories of the trauma. You'll recall that declarative memories associated with a strong emotional event tend to become implicit, or relatively permanent. I'm going to call this state of implicit/procedural memories a *capsule*, primarily because these procedural and emotion-linked declarative memories are stored in a "container" in the exact form in which they were experienced at the moment of trauma. And each of these stored procedural memories is linked to the others, and can act as a cue to them. The procedural memories are subject to being triggered into consciousness by internal or external cues reminiscent of the traumatic event. And all effective psychotherapy must access and open this capsule and its memories *in a safe place* in order to extinguish them.

The Dissociation Capsule:
The Procedural Memory Reservoir

I've defined dissociation as a state of perception of ourselves and the world when we're basically in the freeze response. There are a number of altered states of perception that reflect the state of dissociation. One is the "out of body experience"—actually seeing or looking down on oneself in the memory of the trauma. Some people have attributed this to the idea of the soul literally leaving the dying body and beginning its journey to the afterlife. But this state of perception may also occur in the face of life-threatening trauma sufficient to trigger the freeze/dissociation state. The term for this is *depersonalization*.

Another example is an altered perception of time, usually with time drastically slowing in the face of a life-threatening emergency. "Time stood still" or "my life passed before my eyes" are common ways of describing this dissociative state. "Déjà vu" (the strange looks familiar) and "jamais vu" (the familiar looks strange) are also examples of altered perception of familiarity during the dissociative state. These are examples of *derealization*. Conversion hysteria, as I've noted, is selective dissociation of a body part or region, usually reflecting its participation in a failed act of self-defense. One may not be able to feel the dissociated body part, or it may be painful, numb, paralyzed, or stuck in a bizarre posture. Fugue states, periods of amnesia often associated with confused or highly emotional behavior, also represent states of dissociation.

Dissociative identity disorder (DID) is a controversial but quite real example of severe dissociation. In DID, the individual may have dissociative states or "alters" with distinctly different personalities, different autonomic states, and even different diseases, probably based on the specific state of autonomic dysfunction characteristic of that particular capsule. DID is almost always associated with severe and repetitive physical or sexual childhood abuse.

And finally, as I've said, intrusive thoughts represent repetitive memory intrusions that relate to an unresolved conflict over which we have no or poor control. The conflict always has approach/avoidance features that create the associated state of helplessness. Therefore, intrusive thoughts can be considered to be dissociative in nature, reflecting a freeze state in the face of threat. These obsessive thoughts seem to have a life of their own, emerge with cues, and often surface when we're trying to relax, especially when preparing for sleep. Another term for them is "rumination," like the cow chewing its cud over and over.

Dissociation is basically a state of unresolved traumatic procedural memories that emerge and obliterate or obscure "the present moment." Endorphins are released based on the threat related to the conflict, and also as part of the freeze response (see Key 3). So this state of perception in dissociation is accompanied by an almost drugged alteration of the sense of presence fueled by these endorphins. When these states/symptoms are present, we in fact are actually in the dissociative capsule and not in the present moment.

The content of the dissociative capsule consists of: (1) procedural memories of the body sensations, (2) the patterns of failed defensive movement patterns, (3) the parasympathetic, or even sympathetic, autonomic state, (4) the emotional "feelings" generated by the viscera and gut, and (5) even the declarative memories linked to the emotional arousal of the specific trauma that created the capsule. These "capsules" are brought into consciousness by internal memory cues or external environmental cues that reflect the original traumatic event. They obscure our conscious awareness and therefore our very consciousness. Again, when we are in the capsule, we are not in the present moment— we are locked in the past for the time being. We can't respond to the present world effectively, our sense of self is frozen, and our life is temporarily suspended in space and time (see Figure 8.1).

The concept of the present moment is important for considering the nature of the dissociation capsule. When we're engaged in a task, with thinking, planning, and problem solving occupying our mind, we effectively shut off all of the "noise" in our head from past or ongoing

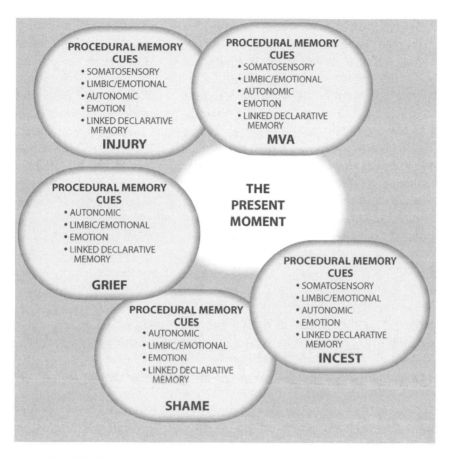

Figure 8.1 The Dissociation Capsule

conflicts. We move through a 1- to 10-second window of time, focused on the present, guided by our autobiographical memories, but aware of the messages of our body and the "feelings" of our emotional state. We in essence are living on the workings of the frontal cortex, the "thinking" brain, and the limbic brain is relatively silent. This state is essentially our creative state, but it also may reflect the process of meditation. If the contents of a dissociation capsule emerge in this state, we immediately leave the present moment and enter the past experiences of that capsule.

The dissociation capsule, obviously, is a metaphor for the state of dissociation in trauma. It isn't visible, tangible, or measureable. But it gives us a template for understanding what this critical concept in trauma actually is, and also what we must do to heal trauma. The inescapable conclusion is that even though the brain contains the driving force for the perpetuation of trauma in somatic procedural memory, one can't extinguish that memory with words alone. Words, of course, are an essential part of the process, and in the end ground the process in acquired wisdom. But one must elicit the messages from the body, the basic content of the dissociative capsule, to complete the process of healing. And then one must find a way to "detoxify" those procedural memories so that they don't continue to perpetuate the process of re-traumatizing the trauma victim. This process can be called "fear extinction." Just as the meaning of the self-protecting role of the tic needs to be extinguished to get rid of the tic, all somatic memory cues need to be extinguished. And if we're going to extinguish procedural somatic messages of fear, we've got to revisit the amygdala.

Reenter the Amygdala:
The Agent of Fear Conditioning

The role of the amygdala must be deeply seated in your declarative memory storage of facts by now. The amygdala, based on early sensory input implying a threat, determines whether we need to experience *fear* and respond by acting defensively. The emotion of fear is something we'd rather not experience if we had the choice. It's basically uncomfortable, and it has many unpleasant implications. But fear is clearly a very important and necessary emotion for survival. And fear conditioning is probably the neurophysiological basis for being traumatized. I'm sure you would all agree that if we somehow became incapable of feeling fear, our basic survival might be seriously compromised. Without the amygdala, there would be no warning that would trigger the fight/flight response. We basically need the capacity to fear, and therefore we need a very functional amygdala.

Neurologist Antonio Damasio has described a very unique patient with the unusual condition of calcification of both amygdalae. Calcium is often deposited in organs where damage to the tissue has occurred, and it is commonly seen in damaged parts of the brain. Damasio's patient had no history of brain damage but did have small partial seizures, the reason she was referred to him. He understood that she clearly had suffered some sort of injury to those specific brain centers—otherwise, they would not be calcified. Knowing the role of the amygdala in arousal and fear, Damasio decided to subject the patient to a series of tests grading her memory, intellect, and emotional stability. The amygdala, of course, plays a role in memory consolidation. Damasio did notice from the start that his patient appeared to be extremely gracious, calm, and imperturbable.

Damasio gave his patient a variety of verbal and pictorial tests, including grading pictures of facial expressions for their benign or threatening demeanor. Surprisingly, the patient had no significant declarative memory problems, as one might have thought she would considering the amygdala's relationship to the hippocampus. Her cognitive function was quite intact. What these tests basically showed was that the patient was *incapable of fear* and could not use visual cues, including the facial expressions of others, to inform her of the presence of danger. But what created this most pleasant and placid of women also placed her in great danger of not having the means to defend herself in a threatening situation. She was quite capable of surviving in the sheltered environment of suburbia but would be at great risk in more dangerous environments, or even in situations where attunement to facial expressions is essential for making decisions about safety versus danger.

Damasio's case is of course of great interest with regard to the role of the amygdala in arousal and survival. But it also provides us with a window of opportunity to observe what implications the absence of amygdala function might have for treating and healing trauma. This patient clearly was incapable of fear, could not experience fear conditioning, and therefore *could never be traumatized!* What meaning might a silent amygdala have for designing therapeutic tools and systems for healing trauma? If one could devise a technique that temporarily down-regulated, inhibited, or turned off the amygdala, one could, during that "sacred space," expose the patient to fear-conditioned procedural memories and their cues and literally extinguish them.

The Essential Ingredient: Inhibiting the Amygdala while Revisiting the Trauma

Guided imagery is an integral part of many forms of psychotherapy, including in the treatment of trauma. One can use imagery to find and enter a place of serenity and safety—a refuge to which the patient can retreat in the face of the eruption of fear that may impair the flow of therapy. Finding an imagined "safe place" is a common technique at the start of any therapy session. One can also use memory-based imagery to find a memory linked to the trauma that one can "work with" in order to gradually diminish its fear-based power. Another technique of "working with" the traumatic thought or memory is *titrating* the access to the memory, or accessing a little piece of traumatic memory at a time before one confronts the whole structure of the traumatic experience. Alternating access to the safe place with accessing a piece of the traumatic memory involves titration—exposure, retreat, exposure, retreat.

But at times, all the efforts at approaching the memory through titration come to naught, and the patient plunges into the core of the memory. This, of course, activates the amygdala and triggers the arousal system of the fight/flight response, in effect consolidating the traumatic memory. The next response by the patient to this arousal in therapy would be to freeze, or dissociate. There's a great deal of concern that dissociating during a therapy session will strengthen the hold that the trauma has on the patient's mind, and thus literally worsen the person's condition. But others believe that some dissociation during a therapy session is inevitable in a trauma victim and is usually controllable. That said, there is general agreement that avoiding profound dissociative episodes in therapy is desirable, as they may interrupt the session.

The best way to avoid dissociation is to inhibit the amygdala from the start as part of the structure of the therapeutic session. From this point on, I will present a working model for effective trauma therapy that I've developed as part of studying the major forms of what I call "somatically based trauma therapy." These techniques have emerged during the past 20 years and are often based on the serendipitous experience of the therapist who "discovered" the technique. After discovery, a speculative neurophysiological rationale is developed to explain how and why the technique heals trauma. The administration of the technique is then finely defined, leading to standardized training programs and certification procedures. In some cases, the techniques are subjected to scientific testing to prove that they are "evidence based."

The growth and proliferation of these "body-based" therapies has been nothing short of remarkable, and many of them have been "offshoots" of existing techniques based on observations by their practitioners. Dramatic claims of rapid resolution of trauma-based symptoms, phobias, panic and anxiety disorders, and especially PTSD have been made and documented in anecdotal and outcome studies, involving dozens to literally thousands of patients. But none of these studies, with the possible exception of EMDR (discussed later), meet the criteria of "controlled," "double-blind," evidence-based research, at least according to the academic behavioral science community. Nevertheless, the undeniable effectiveness of these techniques in clinical office practices has allowed them to burgeon worldwide.

In studying in detail the sometimes ritualistic design of these thera-pies, I have seen in every one of them the feature of in some way in-hibiting, or "down-regulating," the amygdala of the patient in the therapeutic "container," the relationship developed by the attuned therapist with the patient. Understanding that this is informed scientific speculation at best, I am going to explore the dynamics of what I believe constitutes this essential process, or ingredient, for effective trauma therapy and healing.

Banishing Fear: Turning Off the Fear Generator

The problem before us basically is to replicate the status of the limbic brain of Damasio's remarkable patient, who continued to thrive without a danger alarm system. We don't, of course, want to destroy the amyg-dala—which we certainly *could* do with 3-D imaging and a couple of electrodes. We simply want to provide some sort of environment, devoid of threat, where we can revisit cues or memory of the trauma without the interference of fear, panic, or dissociation. It's essentially the same process as ringing the bell and not feeding the dog in order to extin-guish the cue. To do this, we must find and apply conditions, states, environments, signals, or any kind of stimulus or way of being that we know is likely to inhibit, or down-regulate, the amygdala. A good place to start is to look at the very first experience of turning off the amygda-la—the one that occurred in the context of maternal-infant bonding—and figure out a way to replicate it.

Attunement

In Key 4, I discussed the concepts of affiliation between members of a social structure and attunement between mother and her newborn child. You'll recall that maternal-infant bonding promotes the develop-ment of the part of the brain that regulates the autonomic nervous sys-tem and the limbic system. The brain centers involved in this process are the right orbitofrontal cortex (OFC), the anterior cingulate gyrus, and the insula. You'll also recall that an additional role of these brain centers is to modulate and down-regulate the amygdala when the threat is not sufficient to trigger the fight/flight response. These brain centers modulate the limbic brain in order to promote and sustain the critically important state of homeostasis. So if we can somehow "bring on" or activate these limbic centers, we can probably temporarily turn down the amygdala and do some serious therapy and some serious fear extinction.

The process of attunement, or affiliation with another human being, activates mirror neurons between the cingulate and the OFC, creates an empathic environment, and inhibits the amygdala. This sacred face-to-face empathic attunement, then, is a critical environment for trauma therapy to work, just as it is in maternal-infant bonding. In fact, the capacity of psychotherapists to recreate that state with their patients will be a direct measure of their professional success in treating trauma and in psychotherapy in general. Achieving that attunement in the therapeutic setting creates the state of *presence* that is essential for healing— the container in which healing can occur.

The Present Moment

Current psychological literature is filled with books and articles about mindfulness in the therapeutic setting. Mindfulness is basically what we achieve with effective meditation. During effective meditation, one is in a state of awareness of the present while observing thoughts that arise unbidden without pursuing them. One also maintains awareness of the breath, usually guiding it to be rhythmic but continuous and controlled. One may also employ exploration of the *felt sense*, the usually unconscious background somatic and visceral sensations that tell us how we are in the moment. (This is admittedly a vast oversimplification of mindful meditation, but I've chosen those aspects that apply to the business of psychotherapy.) One can say that maternal-infant attunement, mindful meditation, and the effective bond between the therapist and patient all reflect a state of attunement and presence that serves to inhibit the amygdala and restore homeostasis.

In addition, the nature of the breath work during mindfulness also promotes homeostasis and inhibits the amygdala through the influence of the ventral vagal nucleus (see Key 3). In this state of amygdala silence, the threat-based portion of any intrusive thought, traumatic memory, somatosensory procedural memory, or pain will be effectively extinguished. For example, if the patient accesses a body memory of the trauma through scanning for the felt sense, and the amygdala is inhibited through the mutual attuned state between patient and therapist, that procedural body memory will be at least partly extinguished. Without accessing the present moment in therapy, healing of trauma will be difficult indeed. But down-regulating the amygdala usually needs more help than attunement alone can provide. The therapist must also have other tools that specifically facilitate inhibition of the amygdala.

The Power of Ritual

For our purposes, I'm going to define *ritual* as a common practice, developed and approved by a group/congregation/tribe/culture/society, which is given special meaning, often celebrates events, is used as a rite of passage, or actually has healing implications. The commonality of the ritual and its acceptance by the group give it special neurophysiological features and powers, which I believe specifically promote healing from trauma. In more indigenous cultures, ritual is often directed by the tribal shaman and employs trance-inducing states that are aided by rhythm through drumming, chanting, and dance. Occasionally mind-altering substances are used.

The natural affiliation of a select group of people is profoundly enhanced during group rituals. I believe these group rituals actually promote homeostasis and healing of physical and emotional diseases or wounds. As a bonding practice, ritual engages the same limbic brain centers—the OFC, anterior cingulate, and insula—that inhibit and down-regulate the amygdala. The trance state induced is, I believe, quite analogous to therapeutic hypnotic trance in the psychotherapist's office, which is a state during which trauma may heal. With the amygdala inhibited, intrusive thoughts are banished, homeostasis is restored, and healing is promoted. Therefore, techniques with features of ritual, such as those I discuss in the remainder of this Key, are effective tools in providing the emotional and physical healing space that we seek in the therapeutic process.

Empowerment

A traumatic event is basically a life threat that is linked to a state of helplessness. The reasonably resourced person who faces a life threat and thwarts it, either through escape or self-defense, is seldom traumatized and does not develop PTSD or subsequent complex trauma. Posttraumatic procedural memories are extinguished in a state of empowerment. So the introduction of a sense of empowerment in therapy should instill a sense of control and enabling that shuts down the amygdala.

This can be accomplished through a wide variety of environments. Effective imagery, verbal mantras of one's own power, and actual physical replication and completion of failed acts of self-defense in the therapeutic setting dispel helplessness. Creation of artistic models of the event that depict overcoming it and equestrian therapy (where the patient sustains control of a large animal and links its body messages to normal patterns of movement of the human body) are other examples. There are numerous tangible and effective means of recreating mastery of the trauma that will inhibit the amygdala and allow extinguishing of the dissociation capsule contents.

It's very likely that childhood attunement and the lack of childhood trauma facilitate autonomic and emotional stability throughout the one's life, instilling a baseline state of empowerment and self-capacity through adulthood. Conversely, the absence of these empowering traits predisposes the adult to *learned helplessness*. As one's vulnerability to being traumatized is probably based on these early childhood experiences, empowerment plays a huge role in sustaining a state of resiliency and therefore in healing trauma.

Crossing the Cerebral Hemispheres

With the use of fMRIs, we now can view what regions of the brain are in play at any given moment, as well as identify their function based on the experience we are testing. Using this technique, we now know that when the person is perceiving, reliving, or reading a written script of a traumatic event, the right limbic system, including the amygdala, "light up," or come on line. Blood flow and metabolic activity increase. At the same time, when trauma memory is accessed, the left prefrontal cortex (thinking brain) and Broca's area (speech expression) are inhibited, or "shut down." Conversely, while we are meditating (left frontal cortex) or verbalizing nontraumatic information (Broca's area, left frontal lobe), the right limbic system is relatively shut down. Therefore, we can actually use techniques that stimulate each cerebral hemisphere in an alternating pattern to inhibit the amygdala. For instance, humming a song activates the right side of the brain and counting activates the left side, so alternating between humming and counting achieves this pattern in alternate left and right cerebral activation. The other techniques include alternating left and right visual, auditory, or tactile stimuli. Examples include moving a wand or finger back and forth from the left visual field to the right, or wearing headphones that generate a tone or soothing sounds into alternating ears. Touch or vibration may be provided in an alternating fashion to the patient's hands. During all of these exercises, the amygdala will be inhibited, and the window of opportunity for extinguishing the capsule's contents will be provided.

"Completion" of Defense or Escape

Recall for a moment that a tic is a compulsive pattern of movement, especially in the head or neck, that represents a failed motor attempt at self-defense or escape. And recall that the sometimes bizarre posture that's assumed by someone with conversion hysteria represents another example of failed self-protection from a traumatic assault, like the soldiers frozen in the trenches after an artillery bombardment. In both cases, the procedural memory for this failed physical attempt at surviving continues to replicate the movement pattern to no avail. In both cases, the victim froze in the face of helplessness and never went through the act of "completion" of that failed attempt and thus extinction of the traumatic memory. As a result, the unconscious memory retains the threat as being always present, ready to be triggered by any cues to the event. One obvious solution to that dilemma is to allow the aborted movement pattern to emerge and then continue the act to its victorious completion.

This phenomenon of completing the motor act may accompany any form of psychotherapy. It is most commonly elicited when one's "felt sense" of the body is evoked in the therapeutic process. Tracking this subtle "felt sense" through imagery, guidance, or intentional partial movement may result in the "shaking" or other more stereotyped movement responses that extinguish the procedural memory of the trauma and promote healing through literal completion of the self-defensive act.

I could give many examples of this healing process of the freeze discharge, but one from my own life is particularly striking. At age 4, I suffered a very traumatic injury to my left eye when another boy threw an object at me. I had several surgical procedures and required a prosthetic eye. Thereafter I suffered from an embarrassing "nervous tic," squeezing my left eye shut whenever I was under stress. I also had chronic spasm and pain in my levator scapulae on the left side of my neck. At age 60, I came across the work of psychologist Peter Levine, who treated a number of my whiplash victims with a technique called "somatic experiencing," which involves tracking the felt sense in order to initiate and complete the freeze discharge. I asked Levine to show me what he was doing, as many of his patients had experienced dramatic recoveries. In short, accessing my most prominent felt sense resulted in the emergence of a dramatic and totally involuntary movement pattern in my left face, arm, and leg, which I immediately recognized as what my body must have done over 50 years ago at the time of my eye injury—and which was now, in fact, a freeze discharge. Many changes followed, including the complete disappearance of my facial tic and chronic neck spasm and pain.

Restoring Ruptured Perceptual Boundaries

When we start to address such phenomena as auric fields, energy fields, and the perceptual boundaries that surround each of us, we risk seriously offending practitioners who are wedded to "scientific" and "evidence-based" medical science. But many of the somatically based trauma therapies address this phenomenon. Suffice it to say that many psychotherapists in the field are well aware that there are regions in the space surrounding their patients where any form of stimulus—visual, auditory, perceptual—causes anxiety or even panic. In war veterans or victims of sexual assault, this area of arousal sensitivity is usually behind them, and when entering a roomful of people, they position themselves with their back against the wall. People who suffer from whiplash after rear-end auto accidents also may be sensitive to perception of movement or sound behind them. If an accident or attack occurred from one side, the victim will often be sensitive to any stimulus from that side. And in the state of subliminal fear that accompanies this altered spatial perception, low-grade anxiety may occur frequently without the person recognizing the source of the fear and discomfort. Addressing this often-neglected source of arousal cues is an important part of the psychotherapy process.

For example, I tested many of my whiplash victims for sensitivity to visual stimuli by having them look at my face while I passed my hand around their visual field from left to right. Many of them actually flinched when my hand passed their left upper field, the position of the rearview mirror where their gaze had automatically gone at the moment of the rear-end impact. That area of their "perceptual surround" contained unconscious procedural memories for threat. One could refer to this as a "ruptured boundary." The therapist can help extinguish the link between that region of perceptual sensitivity and the threat by gentle sequential stimulation of the visual link in the presence of empathic attunement. Specific examples of this are described in the following section.

The Spectrum of Somatic Psychotherapy

Since the 1990s, there has been a groundswell of discoveries and development of therapeutic techniques for treating PTSD, not by counseling patients or using imaginal exposure, but by guided manipulation of their sensorimotor systems. Many of these techniques were discovered almost by chance by therapists. Others are "spinoffs" of parent techniques. Most of these techniques involve somewhat arcane and ritualistic features that appear bizarre to the traditional psychotherapist. How could tapping on set points on your face or following a rapidly moving finger back and forth with your eyes while imaging a trauma possibly heal your terrible distress? But if one breaks down the specific elements of each technique, one can find what I consider to be the essential ingredients of fear extinction: attunement, ritual, empowerment, alternating sensory stimulation of both cerebral hemispheres, motor acts of completion, and repair of ruptured perceptual boundaries. Although complex trauma may require extended somatic psychotherapy, in many cases the improvement is so dramatic that it defies the usual tenets of trauma therapy. But this very fact is in keeping with the extinction process in classical conditioning.

It's worth mentioning some of the more established somatic techniques. At this point, only eye movement desensitization and reprocessing (EMDR)—the technique I referred to earlier that involves alternating visual, audio, or tactile stimuli—has been studied sufficiently with "evidence-based" scientific protocols to "prove" its effectiveness. Unfortunately, incorporating the body in therapy belies current rationale in the field of psychology. This fact alone makes the likelihood of obtaining grant money for scientific study of these techniques poor. But the effectiveness of these methods in the hands of community-based psychotherapists makes it unlikely that they are going to go away any time soon. Following are brief descriptions of the major techniques. Needless to say, these techniques are far more complex than my descriptions, which provide only a brief rationale for their effectiveness.

EMDR. EMDR is the oldest prototype of somatic psychotherapy. Francine Shapiro developed this technique in the 1990s, produced several scientific papers and books on it, and set up a network of training and certification programs for its use. Since then, its use has spread nationally and internationally, it has been studied extensively, and, although some might disagree, its effectiveness has been largely shown to be "evidence-based." The technique involves moving a hand, light bar, or pointer back and forth while the patient follows it with his or her eyes. One can also provide the stimulus with alternating bilateral sound or vibratory sensations. Statements of self-empowerment are also used. This technique clearly fulfills the criterion of using alternating bilateral cerebral stimulation to shut down the amygdala and extinguish traumatic memories.

Brainspotting (BSP). This technique was devised by David Grand, one of Shapiro's early trainees. He discovered that by slowing down the alternating visual stimulation, he could evoke subtle but reproducible "somatic responses"—usually an eye blink or facial or upper-body twitch. Postulating that these somatic responses represent a perceptual/sensory memory for a traumatic event, he then set about extinguishing this "brainspot" through subtle sequential exposure. He has refined the technique by gradually incorporating subtle nuances of arousal in horizontal, vertical, and near/far representations of the "brainspot." The technique also uses alternating auditory stimuli through earphones during the process. It should be noted that intense attunement is required by the therapist to attain the brainspot, a potential important element for its efficacy.

Somatic Experiencing (SE). This technique, which I mentioned briefly earlier, was developed by psychologist Peter Levine in the 1990s. Levine used the ethological theory of the freeze discharge in animals to devise a technique for eliciting this discharge in traumatized human beings. By following the "felt sense," the patient is able to access somatic sensations linked to a traumatic experience, a process that prompts the emergence of the self-defensive motor action that was aborted during the trauma. This discharge "uncouples," or extinguishes, the retained procedural memories of the trauma and heals the patient. In a sense, the brain now perceives that the threat is gone. SE clearly is based on fear extinction. It is widely used, probably second to EMDR.

Emotional Freedom Technique (EFT). Developed by Gary Craig, EFT is a rather arcane spinoff of Roger Callahan's thought field therapy. It generally falls under the category of energy medicine but has largely been applied to the field of trauma therapy. The esoteric nature of the technique has made it the subject of fierce criticism by the academic establishment, but the methods it uses reflect many of the criteria that I feel are necessary for fear extinction. EFT involves having the patient repeatedly tap acupuncture meridian points on the face and chest with his or her forefinger and middle finger while repeating a mantra-like phrase of self-empowerment. The patient then rotates the eyes to the right and to the left, hums a few verses of a song, counts from 1 to 5, and then repeats the humming. Although these admittedly peculiar actions would seem to defy logical function, they do indeed contain elements that might inhibit the amygdala—empowerment, brain hemispheric crossing (alternating rotation of the eyes; humming to activate the right side and counting to activate the left), and perhaps even ritual. EFT has become a popular adjunctive tool in community-based psychotherapy. Outcome studies of its effectiveness have been quite positive, but controversy still exists in the academic community.

Neurofeedback. Neurofeedback was initially developed as EEG biofeedback in the 1970s and '80s and was primarily used in the treatment of epilepsy. As clinical EEGs began to be computerized, a whole new spectrum of information became available, especially the quantitative measurement of specific EEG rhythms. This allowed precise measurement of different wave frequencies and where they were located. Through the use of sounds and visual cues, neurofeedback therapists became able to change the basic brain-rhythm frequencies and their regional distribution. This allowed therapists to treat such conditions as attention-deficit hyperactivity disorder, depression, substance abuse, minor brain injury, and other brain-based clinical conditions. Results have been promising, with numerous successful outcome studies, though no rigorous controlled studies at this time. Neurofeedback seems to be a useful adjunct to the techniques I've described, as well as to cognitive behavioral therapy and exposure therapy, both of which are mainstream trauma therapy techniques with numerous studies suggesting their validity.

As I mentioned earlier, none of these techniques, except EMDR, are currently "evidence-based" or "proven." But the groundswell of clinician interest in all of them—and the rapid spread in training and use of them throughout the psychotherapeutic community—suggests that movement toward incorporating the body in trauma psychotherapy has just begun and is likely to change the face of treatment.

Endnote

Trauma, in its basic sense, is a corruption of memory. Procedural memories that reflect the body's prior participation in a traumatic event are triggered by any cues of the trauma in daily life. Consciousness is corrupted by the intrusion of past events experienced as if they were occurring now. This deadly dichotomy of perception leads to repeated opening of what I've called the "dissociation capsule," propelling the individual back into a very precise past experience in which amygdala-based terror is a participant. "Then" is "now"—and "now" is then. This is the basic stuff of trauma.

One result of this is the continuous, unpredictable, and intense activation of the autonomic nervous system, with the emergence of exaggerated cycling and loss of homeostasis. Another is the emergence of dramatic somatic symptoms—most commonly, pain in the gut, and in the muscles involved in the failed act of self-defense. These "somatic markers" reflect the body's continuing effort to defend the trauma victim. Further, these somatic memories perpetuate the trauma through repeated kindling and resensitization.

I have made the case that healing, therefore, depends on the extinction of the somatic procedural memories of the trauma. Because fear conditioning is the basic mechanism for establishing trauma, fear extinction must therefore be the essential process of healing. And because fear conditioning is specifically dependent on functions of arousal by the amygdala, fear extinction will only be achieved by inhibiting the amygdala through the theoretical means that I've presented. It takes more than the use of words alone can provide. We must access the messages of the body to complete the healing process. And the wisdom of the body will inevitably lead us there.

AFTERWORD

I am not a psychotherapist; my career in trauma has been as an interested observer, a voracious student, a patient, and an interpreter of the somatic manifestations of trauma in the body. In the process, I have applied these concepts to what is referred to as the "healing of trauma."

We often say we have "cured" a cancer, or a bout of pneumonia or strep throat. Although it's true that we may have healed it, in many cases the susceptibility to the illness still lurks in the body, through our genes or our lifestyles. Similarly, we never "cure" the brain of the effects of trauma. What we *can* do is extinguish critical traumatic procedural memories sufficiently to once again approach autonomic and brain homeostasis. This might well be what we call healing, and depending on the trajectory of our lives, we can build on this new plateau of brain and body health.

Of course, life is rarely consistent or predictable, and new unpleasant or even traumatic events may resurrect dormant procedural memories, interrupting our state of homeostasis and throwing us back into the dysregulation of trauma. But having previously achieved autonomic health, we have reset the set point in our brain, which helps show us the path back to health once again. And this provides us with the gift of insight into what it "feels like" to be whole, present, and regulated. This intrinsic knowledge of "what is"—and the ability to interpret what before had been unavailable to our conscious mind—is the beginning of wisdom. Wisdom is the recognition that the tight muscle on the left side of your neck, however severe, is not a ruptured disc but rather an age-old procedural memory of one of our old traumas. This wisdom shuts off the potential kindling that could have been the next level of this symptom. It also provides us with added perspective, promoting the acceptance and self-understanding that lead to a deep sense of peace and often altruism. Hopefully, our greater understanding of our magnificent brain/body in health, disease, and trauma will empower us on this road to healing and wisdom.

Recommended Reading

Begley, S. (2007). *Train your mind, change your brain: How a new science reveals our extraordinary potential to transform ourselves.* New York: Ballentine.

Damasio, A. (1994). *Descartes' error: Emotion, reason and the human brain.* New York: Avon.

Damasio, A. (1999). *The feeling of what happens: Body and emotion in the making of consciousness.* New York: Harcourt, Brace.

Doige, N. (2007). *The brain that changes itself: Stories of personal triumph from the frontiers of brain science.* New York: Penguin.

Levine, P. (1997). *Waking the tiger: Healing trauma.* Berkeley, CA: North Atlantic Books.

Pavlov, I. (1966). *Essential works of Pavlov* (M. Kaplan, Ed.). New York: Bantam.

Porges, S. W. (2011). *The polyvagal theory: Neurophysiological foundations of emotions, attachment, communication, self-regulation.* New York: Norton.

Rothschild, B. (2010). *8 keys to safe trauma recovery: Take-charge strategies to empower your healing.* New York: Norton.

Scaer, R. (2005). *The trauma spectrum: Hidden wounds and human resiliency.* New York: Norton.

Scaer, R. C. (2007). *The body bears the burden: Trauma, dissociation and disease* (2nd ed.). New York: Routledge, Taylor & Francis Group.

Schore, A. N. (1994). *Affect regulation and the origin of the self: The neurobiology of emotional development.* Hillsdale, NJ: Lawrence Erlbaum.

Selye, H. (1958). *The stress of life.* New York: McGraw-Hill.

Siegel, D. J. (2007). *The mindful brain: Reflection and attunement in the cultivation of well-being.* New York: Norton.

Index

In this index, *f* denotes figure.